Religions.
A Quick Immersion

Quick Immersions provide illuminating introductions to diverse topics in the worlds of social science, the hard sciences, philosophy and the humanities. Written in clear and straightforward language by prestigious authors, the texts also offer valuable insights to readers seeking a deeper knowledge of those fields.

Charles Taliaferro

RELIGIONS
A Quick Immersion

Tibidabo Publishing
New York

Copyediting by Lori Gerson
Cover art by Raimon Guirado

First published 2021

Visit our Series on our Web:
www.quickimmersions.com

ISBN: 978-1-949845-30-3
1 2 3 4 5 6 7 8 9 10

Library of Congress Control Number: 2021948508

Printed in the United States of America.

Acknowledgement

I am grateful to Antoni Comas for inviting me to write this book. I thank Ana Ruiz for her expert editing and guidance. I dedicate this book to each of the 196 students in philosophical theology courses at St. Olaf College during the pandemic of 2020. My hope is that all readers of this book may have the pleasure of encountering such brave, brilliant souls who produced extraordinary work during a profoundly bleak time, while either on campus or learning remotely in Armenia, China, Brazil, Guam or Mexico City.

Contents

Introduction

In a study of over 230 countries, the Pew Foundation's most recent worldwide survey finds that eight in ten people are religiously affiliated. At 84% of the population on this planet, religion is an historically significant mark of identification culturally and personally. Among the four largest religions in terms of size, it is estimated that there are 2.2 billion Christians or 32% of the world population, 1.6 billion Muslims or 15% of the world population, a billion Hindus, and 500 million Buddhists. A very large number, 400 million, practice traditional or indigenous religions as in African traditions, Native American spirituality, Australian aboriginal religions, and so on. In a massive survey of a million people in 163 nations, 50% reported attending a religious service in the last seven days and 56% believe God is active in the world. While the number of those with religious affiliation is a clear majority of the world population, it is estimated that 1.1 billion people have no religious affiliation. That is 16% of the people on earth. The numbers vary across nations; for example, it is rare to find more than 5% of a nation professing to be secular atheists (as opposed to religious atheists, for many practicing Buddhists are atheists), and secular atheists make up over 20% of the population only in China, Vietnam, and South Korea.

The growth and decline of specific religions have been studied; recent research finds that, in 2018-19, 65% of Americans are self-identified as Christian; that is impressive, though in 2008-9 the number was 77%. Still, current sociology of religion estimates that only 4.4% of the US population self-identifies as secular atheists. And in Northern European nations with reputations for being entirely secular (Holland, Sweden, Norway), when measured for church attendance, the evidence is mixed: some profess that, for them, religious practice is a private matter. For example, church attendance in Holland is low among Dutch youth, but a recent study reports that 83% of them pray at least on occasion. Seventy-eight percent of the Swedish population think it is important to have a religious service at death, and 62% think this is important at marriage. In Sub-Saharan Africa, both Christianity and Islam are growing (around 40%

of the population or more each) in terms of public religious practice, and some research supports the prediction that by 2060, four out of ten Christians will be living in Africa.

Some of the growth of secular culture has been through religious persecution. For example, the People's Republic of China has (especially during the Cultural Revolution) criminalized some religious practices and destroyed religious texts. The Soviet Union conducted a vast campaign against religious practitioners with censorship, executions, and imprisonment. And yet there remain diverse religious communities in China today (Christian, Muslim, Buddhist, among others), a revival of Buddhism with thousands of temples being rebuilt and reopened, and evidence of persistent folk religion with ancestor veneration. Sadly, the government is currently seeking to eradicate the Falun Gong movement (which incorporates religious elements) that it labels an "evil cult." Despite persecution in the twentieth century, today in Russia it is estimated that 71% of the population identifies as Russian Orthodox Christians.

Some sociologists of religion have proposed that a reduction of religious practice in some parts of the world (Europe and North America) are due to modern education and contemporary science. This is not obvious. While there are strident, sometimes quite hostile treatments of religion from the standpoint of education and scholarship, this is far from the majority. Indeed, publications like *A Constructive*

Critique of Religion: Encounters between Christianity, Islam, and Non-religion in Secular Societies provides evidence of how educators in Europe and North America promote religious tolerance and inclusion along with constructive criticism.

Is it likely that modern science challenges the credibility of religious belief and practice? From time to time, there has been opposition between science and religion. The persecution of Galileo comes to mind, as does the tension between Darwinian evolution and conservative interpretations of the Bible. But the view that modern science is incompatible with religious faith is strained. A central tenet (the existence of absolute space) in the work of the greatest modern scientist, Isaac Newton, was influenced by eighteenth century theology that posited space as a divine attribute. The co-discoverer of evolution with Darwin, Alfred Russel Wallace, was an early defender of Darwin, but he held that evolution alone needed to be supplemented to explain human spirituality (as well as the emergence of consciousness, mathematics, art, beauty). The point is, though, that Wallace thought evolution was entirely compatible with a religious approach to life. Indeed, Darwinian or evolutionary biology is advanced to describe and explain the emergence of life with all its diversity, but it does not address questions about why the laws of biology, chemistry, and physics are constant over time, why our cosmos exists at all and why it continues to exist from moment to moment.

Further observations about science and religion: one of the leading cosmological theories of the twentieth century, big bang cosmology, was introduced by George Lemaître, a Belgian priest. The director of the Human Genome Project, Francis Collins, sees his work in genetics as supportive of his religious faith.

"As the director of the Human Genome Project, I have led a consortium of scientists to read out 3.1 billion letters of the human genome, our own DNA instruction book. As a [Christian] believer, I see DNA, the information molecule of all living things, as God's language, and the elegance and complexity of our own bodies and the rest of nature as a reflection of God's plan."

Einstein famously wrote that "science without religion is lame, religion without science is blind."

Michael Ruse, a contemporary secular atheist and philosopher of science, is insistent on the compatibility of science and religion. Ruse is addressing science and Christianity, but what he observes can be affirmed of science and Hinduism, Islam, Buddhism, and so on.

"The arguments that are given for suggesting that science necessitates atheism are not convincing. There is no question that many of the claims of religion are no longer tenable in light of modern science. Adam and Eve, Noah's Flood, the sun stopping for Joshua, Jonah and the whale, and much more. But more sophisticated Christians know that already. The thing is that these things are not all there is to religions, and many would say that they are far from the central claims of religion—God existing and being creator and having a special place for humans and so forth."

Ruse goes on to note that religions address important concerns that go beyond what is approachable only from the standpoint of the natural sciences.

"Why is there something rather than nothing? What is the purpose of it all? And (somewhat more controversially) what are the basic foundations of morality and what is sentience? Science takes the world as given. Science sees no ultimate purpose to reality... I would say that as science does not speak to these issues, I see no reason why the religious person should not offer answers. They cannot be scientific answers. They must be religious answers—answers that will involve a God or gods. There is something rather than nothing because a good God created them from love out of nothing. The purpose of it all is to find eternal bliss with the Creator. Morality is a function of God's will; it is doing what He wants us to do. Sentience is that by which we realize that we are made in God's image. We humans are not just any old kind of organism. This does not mean that the religious answers are beyond criticism, but they must be answered on philosophical or theological grounds and not simply because they are not scientific."

There are well published critiques of religion. But I suggest that recent books like Daniel Dennett's *Breaking the Spell*, Sam Harris's *Letter to a Christian*

Nation and *The End of Faith*, and Richard Dawkins'
The God Delusion seem to be both over-confident in
their assertions and very one-sided in their approach
to religion. I have addressed such popular criticism
elsewhere, and the so-called "new atheists" have been
critically addressed by very able defenders of religion
like John Hick, Keith Ward, Chad Meister, and many
others. For example, they point out how Dawkins, a
biologist, seems to mistakenly align religious claims
to biological ones when he writes that "creative
intelligence, being evolved, necessarily arrives late in
the universe, and therefore cannot be responsible for
designing it" (emphasis mine). Many of the religious
philosophers who propose that the origin and
continued existence of the cosmos rests on the nature
and will of God (a creative intelligence, if there ever
was one) contend that God, a necessarily existing
being, is not the product of evolution or is some kind
of spiritually biological thing. The debate over God's
existence is (in part) a debate about the ultimate cause
and continuation of the cosmos and questions why
there should be any cosmos at all in which evolution
(and the sciences themselves) take place. The atheist
philosopher Thomas Nagel suggests that Dawkins
supposes that positing God would be like positing "a
supremely adept and intelligent natural being, with a
super-body and a super-brain…. But God, whatever
he may be, is not a complex physical inhabitant of
the natural world." If God were a complex biological
entity, we might expect an evolutionary explanation

for God, but (as we shall see in this book), God is nothing of the kind.

While Sigmund Freud, the founder of psychoanalysis, proposed that religion is founded on fear, guilt, and underlying psychological neuroses, this has not been supported by studies in psychology and sociology since his time. Herman van Praag, one of the pioneers of biological psychiatry and Professor Emeritus at Albert Einstein College of Medicine in New York, writes:

"I consider receptiveness to religion to be a normal component of the human condition. This view is based on the frequency of the occurrence of this trait and its 'functionality.' It would be difficult to consider a characteristic shared by the majority of human beings as abnormal or pathological. By 'functionality' I mean that religiosity in the life of a religiously receptive person fulfills important functions."

Recent studies in child psychology support the idea that a disposition to religious receptivity starts very early. A senior researcher at Oxford University's Centre for Anthropology and Mind, Justin Barrett, summarizes these studies:

"The preponderance of scientific evidence for the past 10 years or so has shown that a lot more seems to be built into the natural development of children's minds than we once thought, including a predisposition to see the natural world as designed and purposeful and that some kind of intelligent being is behind that purpose. (...) If we threw a handful on an island and they raised themselves I think they would believe in God."

The idea of religion (whether or not it involves a belief in God) has long been held to be natural. Mahatma Gandhi is not alone in claiming that "religion is not a thing alien to us. It has to be evolved out of us. It is always within us: with some consciously so; with others, quite unconsciously."

So, I propose that it is good to immerse yourself in the study of religion in order to learn about the beliefs and practices of those on this religiously diverse planet and there is evidence that being receptive to religion is natural. I also suggest that another reason for immersing yourself in religions involves the meaning of life. You may be interested in religion from the standpoint of culture or politics or art, and not really concerned about the truth or falsity of some or all religions. But if any of the great religions of the world turn out to be true, this has a big impact on who we are and how we live. For example, imagine your principal goal in life is the accumulation of wealth and prestige. If any of the major forms of Buddhism turn out to be true, you have been pursuing an illusion (as we shall see in a later chapter). More positively, if any of the major religions are true, you have an awesome opportunity through prayer and meditation to live in the presence of the sacred (God, Brahman, the Dao, the Compassionate Buddha).

Before getting started on some new enterprise – a new medication or an airplane ride – one is often warned about possible side-effects. If you are going to consider a religious life, there is good news. Many studies by psychologists, biologists, and sociologists have discovered evidence that religious practice can be healthy. Harold Koenig and Harvey Cohen have compiled hundreds of studies on religion and health. Seventy-five percent of them found that religious practice lowers the incidences of disease, strengthens the immune system, reduces stress, lowers blood pressure, and increases life expectancy. Ninety-three studies focused on the relationship of religion and depression: 65% found lower levels of depression among religious practitioners. Of the 68 studies on religion and suicide, 84% of them showed that religious believers have lower suicide rates. Other studies showed some evidence that religious persons are less likely to abuse drugs and alcohol, engage in high risk sexual behavior, and are less likely to divorce.

David R. Williams and Michelle Sternthal observed that religious involvement considerably reduces the risk of mental illness. Richard Layard claims that, overall, people who believe in God are, on average, happier than those who do not.

Freud's student, the Swiss psychoanalyst Carl Jung, took a dramatically different position on religion than his teacher. For Jung, recovery from mental disorders often involved developing a religious perspective.

"Among all my patients in the second half of life... that is to say, over thirty-five - there has not been one whose problem in the last resort was not that of finding a religious outlook on life."

I am not claiming that the above findings are evidence of the truth of religious beliefs. Some false views of reality might lead one to be quite happy and fit. It also may be that what accounts for the health-benefits of religious practice are things like community interaction, being among people of compassion, being in environments where drug abuse is not tolerated, and so on. And we do well to recognize cases of when religious practice produces horrid results: sexual abuse of children by clergy, the shunning of people on grounds of sexual orientation, race, and so on. Because those matters often get more attention in the media than the positive impact of religion, I thought a look at the health-benefits of religion might encourage further reading. It is interesting that these studies support the view of religion advanced by the leader of Tibetan Buddhism, the Dalai Lama, probably the best known, living religious leader in the world (except perhaps for the Pope of the Roman Catholic Church). The Dalai Lama views the religions of the world as types of medicine that can promote a healthy happiness, peace, and compassion.

Earlier I was critical of the philosopher Daniel Dennett for over-stating his claims and being one-sided. But about his endorsing the vital importance of studying religion, I could not agree more.

"It is high time that we subject religion as a global phenomenon to the most intensive multidisciplinary research we can muster, calling on the best minds on the planet. Why? Because religion is too important for us to remain ignorant about. It affects not just our social, political, and economic conflicts, but the very meanings we find in our lives. For many people, probably a majority of the people on Earth, nothing matters more than religion. For this reason, it is imperative that we learn as much as we can about it."

Chapter 1

What Religions are and How to Study Them

As noted in the Introduction, four of the largest religious communities in the world are Christianity, Islam, Hinduism, and Buddhism. Each of these will receive special attention, plus Judaism in chapters two and three. While Judaism has only 14 million practitioners today (2% of the global population), Judaism is important for its own sake (in terms of the origin of Ancient monotheism) but also because Christianity and Islam emerged from Judaism. In this book we will also take some note of primal religions, and attend to Zoroastrianism, Jainism, Sikhism, Shintoism, the Bahai faith, Daoism, and Confucianism. Confucianism has sometimes been classified not as a religion, but as a social and ethical philosophy. One reason for treating it as a philosophy in China, as opposed to a religion, is because of state wariness of religion. Because (it is hoped that) readers of this book need not fear persecution, we will treat Confucianism as a religion in this book due to its rituals, its value system, its promotion of a theory of human nature, and its recognition of the sacred. While some scholars are also inclined to think of Daoism (especially as practiced by sages or intellectuals) as more of a philosophy than religion, but because it too has a worldview, a concept of the sacred, ritual meditation and other practices, it will also be considered a religion here. The official organization of scholars (philosophers, theologians, historians, sociologists, and more) who study religion, the American Academy of Religion (with eight to ten thousand members worldwide), founded in 1909, recognizes Confucianism and Daoism as religions, so we will be in good company.

Before diving into these religions, let us consider a definition of religion. Having a definition of religion is desirable in countries where there are laws about religion. For example, in the United States of America the First Amendment to the Constitution is this: "Congress shall make no law respecting an establishment of religion, or prohibiting the free exercise thereof." Without knowing what counts as a religion, this ruling would not be intelligible. Presumably, a good definition of religion should cover the traditions just cited and we *could* define religion by just listing those traditions recognized as religions. In some dictionaries, colors are defined by giving examples (red, orange, yellow...) and the Supreme Court of the United States has characterized religion as Judaism, Christianity, Islam, Hinduism, and those traditions like them. But such ostensive definitions (an ostensive definition is one that is given by listing examples) do not help us get an understanding of what the religions have in common. In various publications, including dictionaries, I have proposed the following definition of religion:

"A religion involves a communal, transmittable body of teachings and prescribed practices about an ultimate, sacred reality or state of being that calls for reverence or awe, a body which guides its practitioners into what it describes as a saving, illuminating or emancipatory relationship to this reality through a personally transformative life of prayer, ritualized meditation, and/or moral practices like repentance and personal regeneration."

This definition has some advantages over the alternatives. First, it does not identify religion in terms of the belief in one or more Gods. Buddhism is commonly considered a religion, and most forms of Buddhism are non-theistic or atheistic. Besides, there are some who believe there is a God while repudiating religion. The American philosopher Richard Taylor was a strong proponent of theism (he advanced two arguments for God's existence that have received much philosophical attention, pro and con), but he rejected all religions because he believed they were based on fear and superstition. The definition on offer here is also not just a functional one like the one advanced by the founder of sociology, Émile Durkheim, who defined religion in terms of it providing a unified, stable cultural identity which defines authoritative governing codes of conduct. Religions may all, in their different ways, have various functions sociologically, but such a definition does not highlight the fact that all or most religions offer a vision of some ultimate reality or state of being. Sociological definitions focus on only the human dimension of life without taking seriously the claims of some (but not all) religions that our cosmos is created and sustained in being by a transcendent God.

What I suggest is especially important in a definition of religion is to not build-in judgments of the reasonability, truth or falsity, or value of the religion. For example, it would be begging the question if one defined "religious faith" as "believing something you know to be false." In fact, it would be very difficult to create a fair, non-biased definition of religion by focusing on a specific idea of faith. That is because faith, from the standpoint of multiple religions, is highly varied. Faith has been understood as (a) belief and practice based upon evidence and reason, (b) a level of trust that exceeds evidence and reason, (c) a level of trust that is contrary to evidence and reasons, (d) a commitment that does not require belief (I may commit myself to being in a relationship and trust my partner whether or not I confidently believe my trust will always be reciprocated). The definition of religion offered here is neutral on matters of reason and evidence.

One important clarification about using the term "religion": in the definition I propose some persons will be classified as following a religion even though they claim not to be religious. This is true of the famous Protestant, Christian theologian Karl Barth. "Religion is unbelief," Barth wrote in his *Church Dogmatics*, volume one. "It is a concern; indeed we must say that it is the one great concern of godless man. It is the attempted replacement of a divine work by a human manufacture." Barth is drawing attention to his view that Christianity is about a relationship with God through Jesus Christ (the word of God) and not merely about being part of a human institution. Because you are reading a book about religions, as opposed to a work in theology, I simply make note of Barth's terminology and will proceed with the idea that Christianity is a religion even if there are theological reasons for distinguishing religion from a relationship with Jesus of Nazareth. A second case should be noted: there are people today who prefer to think of themselves as spiritual rather than religious. In *The Spiritual Revolution*, Paul Heelas and Linda Woodhead observe:

"Survey after survey shows that increasing numbers of people now prefer to call themselves 'spiritual' rather than 'religious'. Terms like spirituality, holism, New Age, mind-body-spirit, yoga, feng shui, chi and chakra have become more common in the general culture than traditional Christian vocabulary. Even a cursory glance around the local bookshop or a stroll around the shopping centre leaves little doubt that Christianity has a new competitor in the 'spiritual marketplace.'"

That seems right, though it might be observed that Christianity has long had "competition" with other faiths and secular alternatives. But apart from that, it seems to me that self-described "non-religious" persons might find of great interest the spirituality fostered by the great world religions. Yoga (to take just one example listed in this passage) may be appreciated today solely for its health benefits, but one can get a fuller picture of the practice if you explore its Hindu origins. I also suggest that many supposedly non-religious forms of spirituality may have multiple religious roots in which persons are inspired by the Hindu Gandhi's practice of non-violence, the Christian Martin Luther King Jr.'s radical opposition to racism, and so on.

So, how should one study religion? One may use the full range of disciplines available to us: philosophy, history, theology, sociology, anthropology, economics, logic, the natural sciences (physics, biology, chemistry), psychology. Literature can be vital, as there is some sign of religious themes from the earliest human writing. The arts in general (architecture, painting, statues, altars, music…) may enrich one's study. One should also not neglect common sense and the ways that religious practitioners seek to build on or to challenge what many of us think as ordinary features of the world. Many readers of this book probably believe that our individual identities are fundamentally real and enduring in a substantial way. Some forms of Hinduism and Buddhism challenge the ultimacy of this understanding of ourselves.

Perhaps the most important methodological concern is how to weigh what may be called the *insider* or *outsider* perspectives. Do you have to be a religious practitioner in order to really understand the nature of a religion? The philosopher John Lamont has proposed the following:

"This perspective –of the believer– cannot be the same as that of an unbeliever… An unbeliever cannot properly evaluate the reasonableness of Christian faith, because the evidence necessary for such an evaluation is not available to him. The only way for him to find out whether faith is reasonable is to, as far as it lies in him, take the venture of believing."

We should perhaps not reject this too quickly. If our topic was romantic love, it would be hard for a person to understand the nature of romantic love if one had never experienced it. Lamont is also backed up by the most famous twentieth century advocate of mysticism, Evelyn Underhill. In her book, *Practical Mysticism*, she writes about how the mystic who has union with the divine reality has knowledge that cannot be obtained by an outsider:

"Because he [the mystic] has surrendered himself to it [the divine], 'united' with it, the patriot knows his country, the artist knows the subject of his art, the lover knows his beloved, the saint his God, in a manner which is inconceivable as well as unattainable by the looker-on."

While I suggest that some personal exposure to religious life may be an asset, as it would be an asset in the study of religion if you have (at least once) been religious, I do not think it is essential. Although the analogies with romantic love, patriotism, and art are telling, I think that non-religious persons may well be able to understand and critically assess what a religious believer holds about God (Allah or Brahman or the Dao) being awesome, by their experiences of the natural world as awesome. I suggest that so much of religious life is expressed in language that involves things and events we know in non-religious life (the sacred has been described as home, a mountain, the ocean, the sky, the good shepherd, father or mother, the ground on which we stand, light, and so on), that you can grasp the meaning of sacred texts (Hebrew Bible, Christian New Testament, the Qur'an, the Bhagavad Gita) without being a practitioner. We should not underestimate our use of imagination and our capacity to be open-minded.

Another reason for doubting the claim that only "insiders" can understand a religion and its evidence is the fact that over a long history, and today, people voluntarily (freely as opposed to submitting to coercion) convert to a religion from either another religion or no religion at all. In order to convert to a religion by using reason, surely one must be able to grasp some of the evidence for and against a religion. We should also take seriously the long historical record (and contemporary practice) of dialogue and respectful arguments between different religious practitioners. This dialogue is unintelligible without there being a good faith effort by persons successfully understanding one's own and other religions.

Consider several cases of when there have been reasonable cross-cultural understanding and arguments about religion. Probably the most evident and sustained are the arguments and dialogues in India with Hindus, Buddhists, and Jains. Practitioners of each religious tradition would often engage in public debate. They practiced what was sometimes called *Nyaya* which means "the science of reasoning" with rules about structuring arguments and objections. ('Nyaya' is also used to refer to a Hindu school of thought that accepted the authority of the Vedas, something Buddhists reject.)

Disciplined debate sometimes involved debaters being willing to suspend their own beliefs and to adopt (for the sake of argument) the point of view of another religion or philosophy. As most Hindus recognize the reality of a transcendent divine being (Brahman) while Buddhist and Jains do not, the debates included the first exchange on the problem of evil (If God is all good and all powerful, why is there so much suffering?). Nyaya or disciplined debate was distinguished from another practice, *Jalpa*. In the latter case the goal was simply winning. In the West, this is akin to the distinction between *philosophy* (which literally means the love of wisdom) and *sophism* (the art of merely winning). Also in India, during the reign of Ashoka (268-232c BCE), we should note how Ashoka decreed that there should be widespread respect for all religions. So, while Ashoka was a Buddhist, he did not tolerate the persecuting of non-Buddhist religions. In the passage that follows Ashoka is referred to as "Beloved-of-the-Gods":

> "Beloved-of-the-Gods honors both ascetics and the householders [lay people] of all religions... Beloved-of-the-Gods does not value gifts and honors as much as he values this –that there should be growth in the essentials of all religions. Growth in essentials can be done in different ways, but all have as their root restraint in speech, that is, not praising one's religion, or condemning the religion of others without good cause. And if there is cause for criticism, it should be done in a mild way. It is better to honor other religions for this reason. By doing so, one's own religion benefits, and so do other religions, while doing otherwise harms one's own religion,

due to excessive devotion, and condemns others with the thought 'Let me glorify my own religion,' only harms his own religion. Therefore contact (between religions) is good. One should listen to and respect the doctrines professed by others. Beloved-of-Gods desires that all should be well versed in the good doctrines of other religions."

We also note that outside of India there have been sites of profound mutual dialogue between different religious practitioners: the House of Wisdom in Baghdad, the exchanges between Muslim, Jews, and Christians in Spain prior to 1492, the dialogue between Muslim and Christian philosophers in Europe and the Near East after the Crusades. And not to be omitted is the case of Al-Biruni, an eleventh century Muslim philosopher, scientist, geographer, mathematician, who is known as the most fair-minded person in the entire history of ideas to be able to write with great identification and clarity about those who were of other faiths: Hindus, Buddhists, Jains, Zoroastrians, and others. He learned Sanskrit so that he could translate Hindu texts so that Hindus could speak for themselves to Muslims and others.

What is the path forward in this immersion? In the next chapter we will encounter the three major Abrahamic faiths –Judaism, Christianity, and Islam— while taking stock of what are now lesser-known religions, but which were very powerful in the ancient world and in the early common era. (The "common era" is the period beginning in year one of what used to be referred to as A.D. for Anno Domini, the year of the Lord, referring to the birth of Jesus Christ.) Chapter three will consider religions that originated in Asia, and chapter four will look to further religious developments and how to think about religious diversity. Our main study, then, begins with what some philosophers refer to as the Axial Age or the age of values. Over a 600-year period there emerged extraordinary figures who inspired great religious and philosophical traditions. In China in the sixth to fifth centuries BCE there was Confucius, Mencius, Mozi, and Laozi (traditional author of the *Tao Te Ching*) who were (roughly speaking) contemporaries. In India, there emerged traditions that produced Hindu sacred texts, the Upanishads, the Bhagavad Gita; we find Gautama, the Buddha (fifth – sixth century BCE) and the founding of Buddhism; and Mahavira (sixth century BCE) who founded Jainism. In Persia there was Zoroaster (around 1000 to 900 BCE). In Egypt in the reign of pharaoh Akhenaten (fourteenth century BCE), we see the proclamation of monotheism. In Palestine we see the great Hebrew prophets Amos, Hosea, Jeremiah, Isiah, Ezekiel (dating back to the eighth century BCE) and eventually Jesus of Nazareth (death 30-33 CE). In Greece we find Socrates (470-399 BCE), Plato (428-348 BCE), and Aristotle (384-322 BCE). At the end of this book you will find a chronology of figures and events.

In this study, we will explore what some of these great figures and their successors have in common. By way of sketching three points of commonality. First, there is consensus on some version of the golden rule.

"Do not impose on others what you yourself do not desire."

Confucius

"One should never do that to another which one regards as injurious to one's own self. This, in brief, is the dharma. Yielding to desire and acting differently, one becomes guilty of adharma."

Mahabharata (sacred Hindu text)

"He who for the sake of happiness hurts others, who also wants happiness, shall not hereafter find happiness. He who for the sake of happiness does not hurt others, who also want happiness, shall hereafter find happiness."

Buddha (The Dhammapada)

"Love your neighbor as yourself."

Jesus Christ in the Gospel of Mark 12:31

"No man is a true believer unless he desires for his brother that which he desires for himself."

Muhammad (from the Hadith)

Second, great religious figures in the world challenge people not just to follow the golden rule, but to transcend narrow self-interest and, third, all the great religions of the world call on us to be receptive to what calls for reverence.

While this book will focus on religions historically, it should be appreciated that the roots of religion pre-date recorded history. As far back as 100,000 years ago, the Neanderthals buried their dead with food and precious metals. Cro-Magnons, 25,000 years ago, buried their dead with food, ornaments, weapons, and ritual objects. This suggests some idea of life after death, a feature of most, but not all, religions. The reason for our not lingering on these early pre-historic findings is that they call for too much speculation. Anthropologists seek to fill out their portrait of primal religion by studying contemporary societies in Africa, Central and South America, Australia, and elsewhere, that have not made contact with external cultures. But while their work provides some evidence of a natural human disposition to see the world as sacred in some way (possessing meaning and purpose, deserving our reverence), we are on firmer ground when encountering religions and philosophies that produced writing that is accessible to subsequent translation and scholarship.

The Lion-Man

In the 1930s, two archeologists discovered in a chamber in southwest Germany what many believe is one of the earliest-known religious sculptures, dating back to 40,000 years ago. It is an animal shaped sculpture depicting what appears to be a human body and a lion head. Because there is no writing we know of earlier than 5,500 years ago, the nature of the object remains a mystery, but scholars such as Mark Wynn of Oxford University see it as some evidence of a link between the emergence of art, the imagination, and religion.

In our immersion into religions, I propose we avoid what may be called the proof fallacy and stereotyping.

The Proof Fallacy. Those trained in mathematics and logic are accustomed to proof and disproof. One may prove that $1+1 = 2$ is necessarily true because it is based on the law of identity (A is A or everything is itself) and 2 simply is $1+1$, so $1+1 = 2$ is just $1+1 = 1+1$. But when it comes to big views of reality (answering the question about what there is), I suggest that in today's philosophical climate, there is no one picture of all reality that everyone thinks is proven true. Actually, today philosophers, theologians, and scholars are almost always comparing and evaluating what they take to be good or bad arguments in terms of evidence and reason. And this process of using reason does not always exclude the emotions. If we are arguing about a point in religious or secular ethics, different parties may appeal to your compassion, your experience of love and hate. Even the very nature of our thinking and consciousness is currently considered an open question, and not a matter of proof. Consider the following "confession" of Michael Lockwood, who thinks that consciousness is a material / physical process, but note how he thinks this is far from obvious:

"Let me begin by nailing my colours to the mast. I count myself a materialist, in the sense that I take consciousness to be a species of brain activity. Having said that, however, it seems to me evident that no description of brain activity of the relevant kind, couched in the currently available languages of physics, physiology, or functional or computational roles, is remotely capable of capturing what is distinctive about consciousness. So glaring, indeed, are the shortcomings of all the reductive programmes currently on offer, that I cannot believe that anyone with a philosophical training, looking dispassionately at these programmes, would take any of them seriously for a moment, were it not for a deep-seated conviction that current physical science has essentially got reality taped, and accordingly, something along the lines of what the reductionists are offering must be correct. To that extent, the very existence of consciousness seems to me to be a standing demonstration of the explanatory limitations of contemporary physical science. On the assumption that some form of materialism is nevertheless true, we have only to introspect in order to recognize that our present understanding of matter is itself radically deficient. Consciousness remains for us, at the dawn of the twenty-first century, what it was for Newton at the dawn of the eighteenth century: an occult power that lies beyond the pool of illumination that physical theory casts on the world we inhabit."

So, I encourage all of us (readers and writers) to be wary of dogmatism and to be open minded.

Stereotyping. It is easy to make hasty generalizations. A common one among my students is when they say something like "I'm an atheist, so I'm not religious." There are indeed many theistic religions, but not all religions are theistic. As noted earlier, Buddhism is atheistic, and there are forms of Daoism, Hinduism, and Jainism that are not theistic. The most well-known, globally celebrated religious leader today, the Dalai Lama, is an atheist; that is, he denies that there is a divine creator and sustainer of the cosmos. (A brief word on terminology: "atheism," etymologically, means "without God," but I think it is best defined as someone who believes that theism is false. So, an atheist, as opposed to someone who may be called a "non-theist," is someone who has considered theism and claims it is false. The reason for making this point comes to the fore in an analogy. Imagine you have never read or considered the philosopher Hegel, but it turns out that your own philosophy is almost the exact opposite of Hegel's. In this case, I think you would be best described as non-Hegelian but not anti-Hegelian.)

We should pause and challenge a major stereotype. One of the most outrageous and misleading, yet popular, distinctions between so-called Eastern and Western philosophy is that the West is individualistic, materialistic (in the "popular" sense of consumerism and market exchanges), imperialistic, and laced with dualities or polarities of false or illusory oppositions such as male and female, reason and desire, justice and mercy, soul and body, etc. To sum up the West in a single (stereotype) term, it is dualistic ("dualistic" is probably the most abused term in English; it sometimes means philosophies involved in immoral, sexist, superstitious, clearly false and damaging concepts of human persons in which there is a pernicious distinction between the soul or mind on the one hand and the grotesque body on the other). By way of contrast, Eastern philosophy is viewed as relational, non-individualistic, spiritual, democratic, non-imperialistic, holistic (seeing mind and body, male and female, reason and desire, as compatible). And so on.

This portrait is false, but in the spirit of charity, it may be allowed that the above crude portrait has some *highly misleading* yet superficial truth. To offer an example: yes, if by the "West" we mean European and post-Columbian America and those cultures and persons impacted by them, then there has been more stress on individual rights – as found, for example, in the 1689 Bill of Rights, a bill that secured "the freedom of speech and debates in Parliament" and their protection from censure— than one finds during that period of time (the surrounding one hundred years) in China, India, Japan, or Korea. But the "East" has included philosophers who have embraced natural law (see, for example, Dong Zhongshu) and very vigorous ethical and social-political positions that give individual liberty an extraordinarily wide scope. The East shares some of the Western background in terms of pre-linguistic, oral philosophy, and an inheritance of stories of ostensibly supernatural (or at least not-mundane) gods and goddesses not completely different from the world of Homer and Hesiod; you can find philosophers in the East who (as in the West) have held that human beings are naturally oriented to the good (Mencius) or we are naturally drawn to less good, selfish ends (Xunzi); there are cases of what some would call "dualism" (a term that should probably be banished from the language) in the sense that some Eastern philosophers distinguished matter and spirit (as one finds with Ishvarakrishna in which matter is prakriti and spirit is purusha); there are skeptical arguments that predate Descartes' famous challenge when it comes to thinking about radical alternatives—how do you know that you are actually experiencing and interacting with the world as it is or simply dreaming or you are under the influence of an all-powerful, deceitful spirit? Some contemporary philosophers think that radical skepticism is an exclusively Western produce: this is demonstrably false. See the work of Nagarjuna.

You might think of karma and reincarnation as distinctively "Eastern," but Western thinkers such as Pythagoras and Plato may be attributed with belief in reincarnation that is determined (as with karma) by merit. You may think that, after the advent of Christianity, the West is exclusively concerned with the existence or non-existence of God as a Creator and person-like as opposed to the monism (all is one) of the East. But the West has philosophers who embrace forms of monism (Spinoza), and while the East has its monists (Shankara), it has its theists or theistic-like counterparts (Ramanuja). In many areas, including logic, philosophy of mind, aesthetics, epistemology, metaphysics, political theory, you can find some parallels: for example, Machiavelli might be favorably compared with Han Feizi or Kautilya.

If you do a close study of the main currents of Eastern philosophy, you will cover much of the ground of philosophy in the West, and vice-versa, but of course the history of culture and philosophy East and West has many significant, particular features that do not admit translation or parallels. The history of philosophy and religion on the Korean peninsula is, for example, unique in world history. The Japanese drawing on (or importing of) Chinese philosophy and culture also seems unparalleled (it is not sufficiently similar to the Roman appropriation of Greek philosophy and culture for the comparison to be interesting).

Nevertheless, please beware of facile, simplistic summaries on the web about "the difference between Eastern and Western philosophy." A random search came up with this depiction [I put in quotes but I have also paraphrased] of East and West: "The West involves the rational, scientific, and logical. Western philosophy is principally focused on discovering what is true. Eastern philosophy is more concerned with balance, the intuitive, and the interior or spiritual." But if that is so, how does one account for the extraordinarily developed work on logic in India or the scientific advances in China altogether pre-dating the West (the invention of gun powder, the compass, paper, etc.), the great debates between different schools of Buddhism, as well as the rational, fine-tuned, highly analytic arguments one finds in Buddhist and Hindu philosophers as they debate what is true and reasonable? As for intuition, one finds all kinds of appeals to what is self-evident or appears true to us through different faculties, and there is even a major movement in the West in ethics and the theory of knowledge known as intuitionism.

More briefly, I suggest a simple, positive goal we should strive for in our immersion: let us treat the religions and philosophies the same way as we would like our own to be treated. This may be termed the golden rule of inquiry.

Chapter 2

Abrahamic Religions: Judaism, Christianity, and Islam

Judaism, Christianity, and Islam are referred to as *Abrahamic* because they trace their history back to the Hebrew patriarch Abraham (sometimes dated to the twentieth century BCE). Abraham is revered as the father of faith. He followed the command of God to leave his homeland, the powerful city of Ur in Mesopotamia, to settle in a new land and to father children who would further populate the earth. From the Book of Genesis:

"Now the Lord said to Abram [later to be called Abraham], 'Go from your country and your kindred and your father's house to the land that I will show you. I will make of you a great nation, and I will bless you, and make your name great, so that you will be a blessing." (Genesis 12:1)

Abraham's first child was Ishmael, whose mother was the Egyptian handmaid Hagar; the mother of his second son, Isaac (meaning he laughs/will laugh) was his wife Sara (later Sarah) who laughed when it was prophesied that she and Abraham would have a child, given their old age. The children of Israel (roughly translated as one who wrestles with God) or the Jews trace themselves back to Abraham and Sarah. From the Book of Isaiah:

> Consider Abraham your father and Sarah who gave you birth. When I called him he was the only one but I blessed him and made him numerous." (Isiah 51:2)

Christians believe that Abraham is an ancestor of Jesus Christ through Isaac, while Muslims believe that Abraham is an ancestor of the Prophet Muhammad through Ishmael.

There are many stories about Abraham in Genesis, but the most haunting is the story of the binding of Isaac.

> It happened some time later that God put Abraham to the test. 'Abraham, Abraham' he called. 'Here I am,' he replied. 'Take your son, your only son, your beloved Isaac, and go to the land of Moriah, where you are to offer him as a burnt offering on one of the mountains I shall point out to you.'" (Genesis 22:1-2)

Abraham responds in faith, prepared to make this sacrifice. An angel intervenes:

But the angle of Yahweh called to him from heaven. 'Abraham, Abraham!' he said. 'Here I am,' he replied. 'Do not raise your hand against the boy,' the angel said. 'Do not harm him, for now I know you fear God. You have not refused me your own beloved son.'" (Genesis 22:11-12).

The Hebrew term for "Here I am" is *hineni*, a term that re-appears multiple times in scripture to indicate one's radical availability to God. Over the centuries this story of Abraham and Isaac has had multiple interpretations: some propose that the whole point is that God does *not* require or allow child sacrifice; others propose that God could require child sacrifice but elects not to; a related interpretation is that the religious duty to obey God transcends ethics. In any case, Jews, Christians, and Muslims trace themselves back to the profound Abrahamic trust in God's holiness – one should trust in the supreme goodness of God, being willing to sacrifice (in the sense of offering) to God one's life. The term "Muslim" is derived from Arabic for one who submits, in this case to God or Allah.

The Hebrew Bible, the Christian Old Testament and New Testament, and the Qur'an, are monotheistic insofar as they affirm that there is one God, and they reject polytheism (the belief that there are many gods).

Since the seventeenth century, "theism" has been the common term in English to refer to their central concept of God. According to the classical forms of these faiths, God is the one and sole God who created and sustains the cosmos. The vast majority in the Abrahamic tradition affirm that God created the cosmos out of nothing (*ex nihilo*), but a minority of philosophical theists hold that the cosmos has always existed but depends for its existence upon God's conserving, creative will. Creation from nothing means that which is created was not created by God shaping or using anything pre-existing or external to God. The cosmos depends upon God's conserving, continuous will the way light depends on a source or a song depends on a singer. If the source of the light goes out or the singer stops singing, the light and song cease (perhaps allowing that there might be a temporary glow or echo, but that is it). Traditionally, the creation is not thought of as a thing that an agent might fashion and then abandon; the idea that God might make creation and then neglect it the way a person might make a machine and then abandon it is utterly foreign to theism.

In these religions, God is said to exist *necessarily*, not *contingently*. God exists in God's self, not as the creation of some greater being (a super-God) or force of nature or evolution. God is also not a mode of something more fundamental, the way a wave is a mode of the sea or a dance is a mode of movement. The cosmos, in contrast, exists *contingently* but not *necessarily*—it might not have existed at all; God's existence is unconditional insofar as it does not depend upon any external conditions, whereas the cosmos is conditional.

Theists hold that God is, rather, a *substantial reality*: a being not explainable in terms that are more fundamental than itself. God is without parts, that is, God is not an aggregate or compilation of things. Theists describe God as holy or sacred, a reality that is of unsurpassable greatness. God is therefore also thought of as perfectly good, beautiful, all-powerful (omnipotent), present everywhere (omnipresent), and all-knowing (omniscient). God is without origin and without end, and everlasting or eternal. Because of all this, God is worthy of worship and morally sovereign (worthy of obedience). Finally, God is manifested in human history; God's nature and will is displayed in the tradition's sacred scriptures.

Arguably, the most central attribute of God in the Abrahamic traditions is *goodness*. The idea that God is not good or the fundamental source of goodness would be akin to the idea of a square circle—an utter contradiction.

Theists in these traditions differ on some of the divine attributes. Some, for example, claim that God knows all future events with certainty, whereas others argue that no being (including God) can have such knowledge. Those who believe that the future is open for future, unpredictable free choices are called open theists. Some theists believe that God transcends both space and time altogether, while other theists hold that God pervades the spatial world and is temporal (there is before, during, and after for God). But it is largely in their views of God's special revelation that the three monotheistic traditions diverge. Let us look at each of these traditions separately highlighting one or more historically significant figures or themes in the different traditions. But first, let us note how each of the Abrahamic faiths understand religious language.

Some of the language in the sacred texts of the Abrahamic faiths employ human attributes when describing God / Allah. God is depicted as sitting on a throne or having eyes or having arms or as being a father or mother. Virtually no representative of these traditions takes this language literally, any more than they take descriptions of God as a fortress or mountain literally. The danger of anthropomorphism (inappropriately assimilating something nonhuman to human form) was not unknown in the ancient world. The Greek philosopher Xenophanes, who thought God lacked any material form, criticized the tendency to picture God in one's own image.

> The Ethiops say that their gods are flat-nosed and black,
> While the Thracians say that theirs have blue eyes and red hair.
> Yet if cattle or horses or lions had hands and could draw,
> And could sculpt like men, then the horses would draw their gods
> Like horses, and cattle like cattle; and each they would shape
> Bodies of gods in the likeness, each kind, of their own.

Jews, Christians, and Muslims have indeed used human attributes in referring to God, but virtually all of them take such attributes to be metaphors or invoking analogies. Because God does not have eyes in a literal sense, to say that "the eyes of the Lord range throughout the earth" (2 Chronicles 16:9) is not to claim that there are divine eyeballs floating around our planet. It is, rather, to claim that God's omniscience encompasses all that there is; there are no facts about you or any creature on our planet or anywhere that is unknown to God. Moreover, when philosophers in the Abrahamic traditions use terms univocally (in the same sense) to describe God and humans (for example, the meaning of the term "know" is the same in these two claims: you know your pain and God knows your pain), they recognize the different modes involved (you know you are in pain due to your brain and central nervous system whereas God's knowledge is not mediated by God's biological constitution).

One more important observation about interpreting sacred texts: each of the Abrahamic traditions understand God to be holy, just and merciful, and thus worthy of worship. Consider, for example the opening of the Qur'an (called the Al-Fatihah):

> 1:1 Praise be to Allah, the Lord of the worlds,
> 1:2 The Beneficent, the Merciful,

1:3 Master of the day of Judgment.

1:4 Thee do we serve and Thee do we beseech for help.

1:5 Guide us on the right path,

1:6 The path of those upon whom Thou hast bestowed favours,

1:7 Not those upon whom wrath is brought down, nor those who go astray.

Given this exalted understanding of God, how should passages of sacred texts be interpreted when it appears that God has commanded something unjust and not at all merciful? In the next section, when we become immersed in Islam, we will consider a vexing passage in the Qur'an that has been used to justify violence. For contemporary Jews and Christians, problematic texts include the brutality of the conquest of people whose land the Jews will inherit (Joshua 10:16-45), the condemnation of homosexuality (Leviticus 18:22), and the tolerance of slavery. Today, many religious practitioners will interpret such passages as highly conditioned by ancient values: the conquest narratives have been interpreted as either a matter of hyperbolic exaggeration or as reflecting an all too human (and not divine) practice, the prohibitions of homosexuality (which are few in number) have been interpreted as not referring to cases of mature, committed same-sex relations, whereas the failure to condemn slavery reflected the fact that in the ancient world it is hard to find more than a few persons who condemned slavery. The point to keep in mind as we look more closely at the Abrahamic traditions is that these are living traditions in which religious followers can engage in innovation and progress in their interpretations of their sacred texts.

Judaism

Traditional Judaism is strictly monotheistic and it portrays God as uniquely calling out the people of Israel to be a just and holy people – a blessing to a world that will itself be blessed: 'I will bless those who bless you, and the one who curses you I will curse; and in you all the families of the earth shall be blessed.' (Genesis 12:3) This monotheism is underscored reverentially by the focal point of morning and evening Jewish prayer services – the Shema Yisrael: 'Hear, O Israel: The LORD our God, the LORD is one.' (Deuteronomy 6:4)

The personal nature of and relational dimensions to this one God are also emphasized in another central prayer of Jewish liturgy – the Amidah or 'Standing Prayer' which includes the following lines:

> We acknowledge You as Lord, our God, ever our ancestors' God, Rock of our lives, our saving shield in every generation. We thank You and recount Your praises – for our lives

entrusted to Your care, for our souls in Your charge, for Your miracles daily with us – continual marvels and bounties, morning, noon, and night! The Good whose mercies never lapse, Merciful Author of unceasing favors, we ever trust in You.

There are many elements that stand out in this prayer, beginning with the importance of a collective acknowledgement. The prayer begins with 'we,' not 'I'. Addressing God as 'You' implies that God is a person or person-like or personal rather than an impersonal principle or universal force. The prayer places the acknowledgement of God into a familial, generational (or ancestral) lineage. The prayer thus evokes sacred history. Interestingly, the prayer's driving force is praise, gratitude, an expression of trust, and recognition of past divine guidance and provision, rather than petitionary (involving an invocation for divine favor in the present and future). God is encountered not as a brute, omnipotent force who requires placation; rather, God is addressed as the Good and the Merciful. (In reverence to the Almighty, many Jewish people do not spell out the term 'God' but rather use 'G-d'.) The Hebrew Bible contains some shockingly personal elements in God's relationship with the people of Israel; for example, in Isiah 43:4 a prophet declares this word of the Lord: "I love you." In the Song of Songs, God's relationship with creatures is portrayed as an erotic romance.

From the standpoint of Judaism, God's principal manifestation was in leading the people of Israel out of bondage in Egypt to the Promised Land (Canaan) as recounted in *Exodus*. This "saving event" is commemorated perennially in the yearly observation of Passover. The tradition places enormous value on community life, a life displayed in the Hebrew bible as a covenant between God and the people of Israel. The more traditional representatives of Judaism, especially the Orthodox, adopt a strict reading of what they take to be the historic meaning of the Hebrew scripture as secured in the early stages of its formation. Other groups, like the Conservative and Reform traditions, treat scripture as authoritative but do not depend on a specific, historically-defined interpretation of that scripture. Although there is some lively disagreement about the extent to which Judaism affirms an afterlife of individuals, historically, Judaism has included an affirmation of an afterlife (Ezekiel 37:1-14).

The first five books of the Hebrew Bible (Genesis, Exodus, Leviticus, Numbers, Deuteronomy) are called the Torah ("teaching"). Genesis opens with God creating ("In the beginning God created heaven and earth" Genesis 1:1) a good cosmos ("and God saw that it was good" 1:10). The first humans, Adam and Eve, are to flourish in a covenant with God, but when they break this covenant (harmony) by disobedience, they are exiled from Eden or paradise. While some Jews, Christians, and Muslims treat the narrative of original, human disobedience as historical (or as literal truth), some treat the narrative as a parable or mytho-poetic way of expressing the idea that there was some primordial turning away from God or the sacred. Subsequent covenants with God include the covenant with Noah after a great flood (Genesis 6-9), the covenant with Abraham (chapter 12), and the covenant with Moses or the Mosaic covenant (Exodus 20). It is in the Mosaic covenant that we find the Ten Commandments:

And God spoke all these words:

"I am the Lord your God, who brought you out of Egypt, out of the land of slavery. You shall have no other gods before me."
II "You shall not make for yourself an image in the form of anything in heaven above or on the earth beneath or in the waters below. You shall not bow down to them or worship them; for I, the Lord your God, am a jealous God, punishing the children for the sin of the parents to the third and fourth generation of those who hate me, but showing love to a thousand generations of those who love me and keep my commandments.
III. "You shall not misuse the name of the Lord your God, for the Lord will not hold anyone guiltless who misuses his name.
IV. "Remember the Sabbath day by keeping it holy. Six days you shall labor and do all your work, but the seventh day is a sabbath

to the Lord your God. On it you shall not do any work, neither you, nor your son or daughter, nor your male or female servant, nor your animals, nor any foreigner residing in your towns. For in six days the Lord made the heavens and the earth, the sea, and all that is in them, but he rested on the seventh day. Therefore the Lord blessed the Sabbath day and made it holy.

V "Honor your father and your mother, so that you may live long in the land the Lord your God is giving you.

VI "You shall not murder.

VII "You shall not commit adultery.

VIII "You shall not steal.

IX "You shall not give false testimony against your neighbor.

X "You shall not covet your neighbor's house. You shall not covet your neighbor's wife, or his male or female servant, his ox or donkey, or anything that belongs to your neighbor."

Some observations: these commands constitute a covenant between God and God's people. A covenant is different from a contract insofar as covenants involve agreements that define one's very identity (like a marriage), whereas contracts can be impersonal (like a commercial exchange in a market). In this covenant, it begins with a positive affirmation that God is the one who liberates those in captivity, it affirms the good of the Sabbath, and it positively affirms the good of children honoring their parents, though many of the commands are formulated in terms of prohibitions: do *not* commit idolatry, do *not* defile God's name, do *not* murder, commit adultery, steal, and so on. The British Romantic poet William Blake lamented a spirituality of negation; in his poem "The Garden of Love" he describes a chapel with a closed door and "Thou shalt not" written above the door. However, the negations or prohibitions in the commandments would make little sense without there being a positive conception of the relevant goods. A prohibition of adultery would make no sense unless based on a belief in the goodness (or sanctity) of marriage, unless one had a positive conception of property, a prohibition against stealing would make no sense, and so on. Describing God as jealous may seem odd, especially if one thinks of the harm that can come from jealousy. But are all forms of jealousy unhealthy? Imagine a parent-child relationship in which the parents have been respectful, loving, generous, nurturing but instead of their children returning such love, they devote themselves to worshiping a cruel neighbor who exploits them. This might be a case in which it would be odd if the parents did not feel some jealousy (maybe even anger). The notion that the God of the cosmos may be jealous if you devote yourself to worshiping something or someone less than God reveals a

God who is committed to a relationship with God's people. In such a context, belief in God's jealousy may be part of believing in God's care and love.

The Covenant with Noah

The covenant with Noah is deeply important for the understanding of God's providential role in creation from an Abrahamic perspective. The story of a world flood and God's rescuing some chosen people and animals in an ark is treated as God's punishment of human wickedness. After the flood God shows mercy to humans by the foreswearing of a comprehensive, immediate punishment of wickedness in this life. It is in light of this covenant that Biblical teachings that the wicked will perish and the faithful prosper come to be treated as aspirational (we should so live such that the faithful flourish and the wicked do not) or eschatological (that is, concerns the end times or an afterlife). From an Abrahamic perspective, God still works within human history through prophets and (in some cases) providential events (the miraculous), but strict, immediate, divine punishment of wrongdoing is renounced. As Judaism evolved nearer the emergence of Christianity, there arose the hope for the coming of the Messiah, a King in the line of David who would usher in a time of peace, prosperity, and a deliverance from enemies.

Judaism is an ethnic religion that has rarely engaged in missionary outreach to encourage conversion. Jewish history includes a golden age (Kings David and Solomon), horrific calamities such as being conquered by the Babylonians and many of the people being exiled ('the Babylonian captivity'), the siege of Jerusalem and destruction of the Temple in 70 CE, the waves of persecutions historically, culminating in the Holocaust or the Shoah in which six million Jews were killed in German-occupied Europe. The religious response to this tragedy has been to hold steadfast to traditional Judaism or to radically revise the belief in an all good, omnipotent God. Judaism as it is practiced through much of the world today stresses the importance of family and community.

Throughout the Hebrew Bible there is an ongoing exhortation to the people of Israel to personally restore themselves into a relationship with God, and not to be distracted by religious ritual or worldly affairs which can themselves become idols. "If my people who are called by my name humble themselves, pray, seek my face, and turn from their wicked ways, then I will hear from heaven, and will forgive their sin and heal their land" (2 Chronicles 7:14); and "I desire steadfast love and not sacrifice, the knowledge of God rather than burnt offerings" (Hosea 6:6). And then in Isaiah:

Look, when you fast and still do as you like,
And drive all your workers hard –
Fast but go on fighting,
Pressing your pleadings, brawling...
Is that the fast I want,
Folk tormenting themselves,
Heads bowed like a bulrush,
Lying in sackcloth and ashes?
Is that what you call a fast,
A day to please the Lord?
No, this is the fast I want:
Unlock those evil fetters,
Loose the traces of the yoke,
Free the downtrodden,
Break off every yoke!
Share your food with the hungry,
Bring home the wretched poor.
Clothe the naked when you see him,
And do not make yourself invisible
To your own flesh and blood. (from Isaiah 58)

This passage is read during Yom Kippur (also known as the Day of Atonement), a holy day for repentance, fasting, and intensive prayer. In this teaching from Isaiah, nothing can be hidden from God; there is no use hiding behind visual, pious rituals, while trying to be invisible to God and simply not available to the poor and the dispossessed. As we shall see in the context of other religious traditions, there has sometimes been tension between a stress on ritual and a stress on inward, authentic spiritual wellbeing.

Another important element in Judaism is the role of wisdom as a divine gift and as revealing God's will. In the book of Proverbs we find a creative expression of wisdom herself:

> The LORD created me at the beginning of his work,
> the first of his acts of long ago.
> Ages ago I was set up,
> at the first, before the beginning of the earth.
> When there were no depths I was brought forth,
> when there were no springs abounding with water.
> Before the mountains had been shaped,
> before the hills, I was brought forth—
> when he had not yet made earth and fields,
> or the world's first bits of soil.
> When he established the heavens, I was there,
> when he drew a circle on the face of the deep,
> when he made firm the skies above,
> when he established the fountains of the deep,
> when he assigned to the sea its limit,

so that the waters might not transgress his
command,
when he marked out the foundations of the
earth,
then I was beside him, like a master worker;
and I was daily his delight,
rejoicing before him always,
rejoicing in his inhabited world
and delighting in the human race. (8:22-31)

This extoling of wisdom hints at an intersection
between religion and philosophy. "Philosophy" is
derived from the Greek term for love (*philo*) and
wisdom (*sophia*). Both Ancient Judaism and Ancient
Greek philosophy praised wisdom as a way to
apprehend values and as a way to live. Wise persons
not only know what is valuable (what should be loved
and by how much), they seek to embody in their lives
a response to values. It is this wisdom tradition (in
Latin the *sapiential* tradition) that over time fills
out an ethic of virtue (valorizing courage, justice,
integrity, self-mastery or temperance, prudence
or wisdom in practical matters) and vice (vanity,
uncontrolled anger or rage, lust, begrudging envy,
sloth, greed, gluttony or self-indulgence).

The wise prophets spoke regularly and
impassionedly about social issues, notably in terms of
care and concern for the poor and disenfranchised. The
Mosaic notion of justice incorporated an obligation to
the disadvantaged and marginalized. Throughout the

Torah one finds mention of safeguarding widows, orphans, and strangers (Exodus 12:49; 22:21-22; Leviticus 23:22; 25:35-36; Deuteronomy 15:7-8; 24:17). Mandates to care for those in need include Israelites and non-Israelites, and it matters not what one's station in life is or how one ended up in dire straits. And there are consequences for ignoring these directives for the disenfranchised. 'Cursed is the man who withholds justice from the alien, the fatherless or the widow.' (Deuteronomy 27:19)   In the latter prophets, mandates for social justice continue. The prophet Isaiah:

> The Lord will enter into judgment
> with the elders and princes of his people:
> "It is you who have devoured the vineyard,
> the spoil of the poor is in your houses.
> What do you mean by crushing my people,
> by grinding the face of the poor?"
> declares the Lord God of hosts. (3:14-15)

Divine concern for justice is perhaps best memorialized in the words of the prophet Amos:

> But let justice roll down like waters,
> and righteousness like an ever-flowing stream. (5:24)

Prior to the Jewish-Roman Wars beginning in 66 CE, Jews were tolerated in Rome and in important cities like Alexandria in Egypt, a renown site for philosophy and learning. Chief among Jewish philosophers at the time was Philo of Alexandria (20 BCE-50 CE), a contemporary of Jesus Christ (with whom he had no contact). Philo's work was influential in terms of both Jewish and Christian ways of interpreting scripture. It is from Philo that subsequent commentators treated large portions of the Bible as allegories. In Genesis, chapter one, when the creation takes place over six days, Philo points out the fitting nature of six as a perfect number (a perfect number is equal to the sum of its divisors, including one but not including itself; 1+2+3=6; 6 is the smallest perfect number). It was in the spirit of Philo that subsequent commentators would treat the Biblical story of Jonah being swallowed by a giant fish as an allegory about God delivering people from evil. More importantly, Philo was the first major Jewish philosopher to address the relationship between Greco-Roman philosophy and the Hebrew Bible. Putting it differently, how should one think of Moses and Plato or, as an early theologian put it, what does Athens (the birthplace of philosophy) have to do with Jerusalem (a city holy to Jews)? Philo sought for harmony, highlighting when Platonic and Neoplatonic thought had monotheistic currents, and taught about virtues that could reinforce claims from the Hebrew Bible.

In the following passage one can observe how Philo is a philosopher in the wisdom tradition, beseeching us not to foolishly pursue worldly glory based on passing wants, but to seek out the higher call of a God of virtue who is not prey to greed.

"We must mention the higher, nobler wealth, which does not belong to all, but to truly noble and divinely gifted men. This wealth is bestowed by wisdom through the doctrines and principles of ethic, logic and physic, and from these spring the virtues, which rid the soul of its proneness to extravagance, and engender the love of contentment and frugality, which will assimilate it to God. For God has no wants, He needs nothing, being in Himself all-sufficient to Himself, while the fool has many wants, ever thirsting for what is not there, longing to gratify his greedy and insatiable desire, which he fans into a blaze like a fire and brings both great and small within its reach. But the man of worth has few wants, standing midway between mortality and immortality."

The long history of Judaism from the time of the Jewish diaspora onward, triggered by the traumatic destruction of the Temple in 70 CE, has multiple layers. Of the many who helped shape Judaism historically, Maimonides (1138-1204) is a towering figure. He sought to stabilize the central teachings of Judaism and establish the great centrality of study for an observant Jew. In his *Laws Concerning the Study of the Torah*, Maimonides writes:

> The time allotted to study should be divided into three parts. A third should be devoted to the written law — that is, the Bible; a third

to the oral law; and the last third should be spent in reflection, deducing conclusions from premises, developing implications of statements, comparing dicta, studying the hermeneutical principles by which the Torah is interpreted, until one knows the essence of these principles and how to deduce what is permitted and what is forbidden from what one has learned traditionally. This is termed Talmud.

Maimonides (who is sometimes known as Ramban) has inspired observant Jews to study the Torah and Talmud daily. The Torah refers to the Five Books of Moses (Genesis, Exodus, Leviticus, Number, and Deuteronomy), but it is often extended to cover all books from Genesis to Chronicles in the Hebrew Bible. The Talmud ("teaching" or "study") was published in the third century to bring together past and contemporary commentary on Jewish law and practice. Maimonides identified thirteen principles of Jewish faith. The thirteenth explicitly affirms life after death:

I believe by complete faith that there will be a resurrection of the dead at the time that will be pleasing before the Creator, blessed be His name, and the remembrance of Him will be exalted forever and for all eternity.

Maimonides had warm relations with Muslims, and actually served as a physician to the Kurdish Muslim Saladin who conquered Jerusalem (freeing it from Christian crusaders) in 1187. It is from Maimonides that we get some popular sayings such as: "Give a man a fish and you feed him for a day; teach a man to fish and you feed him for a lifetime." And: "It is better to acquit a thousand guilty persons than to put a single innocent one to death."

More recently, in the twentieth century, two religiously observant Jewish thinkers standout. The first is Martin Buber (1878–1965).

Buber was a brilliant Jewish philosopher whose influence is still very much in evidence. Buber stressed the primacy of personal relationships over impersonal relations, which he formulated in terms of "I-You" or "I-Thou" relations rather than "I-it" in which you treat things and persons as less than personal. The nineteenth and twentieth century fostered highly mechanized ideologies and practices (Marxism, unfettered capitalism, fascism) that overshadowed the nature and value of the individual person. Buber's religious response may be called *personalism*.

"If I face a human being as my Thou, and say the primary word I-Thou to him, he is not a thing among things, and does not consist of things. This human being is not He or She, bounded from every other He and She, a specific point in space and time within the net of the world; nor is he a nature able to be experienced and described, a loose bundle of named qualities."

For Buber, it is in personal relations where (and when) God is encountered. "When two people relate to each other authentically and humanly, God is the electricity that surges between them." In 1925, Buber translated the Hebrew Bible into German, in collaboration with Franz Rosenzweig in Frankfurt. Buber promoted using the scripture, not as a discursive tool to get descriptive knowledge of God, but to use as a means of developing interpersonal relations in community and in the encounter with God through prayer, meditation, confession, repentance, reconciliation. From his perspective, God cannot so much be *described*, as *addressed*, in prayer and Godly action.

In addition to Buber, consider Abraham Joshua Heschel (1907–1972). Heschel was a Jewish philosopher, public intellectual, rabbi, and civil rights activist. Though born in Poland and educated in Germany, he fled Europe in the Second World War and taught in America for the rest of his life. He is one of the twentieth century's most widely read and respected interpreters of Jewish thought, especially among non-Jewish readers. One of his lifelong pursuits is distinguishing the God of the Hebrew Bible — present, alive, invested in people — from the more abstract, disinterested God of Greek metaphysics. Heschel's writing is stirring, brimming over with a life-affirming call to fullness of life. He spoke about living with "radical amazement," founded on a profound, sustained realization of life as an awesome gift.

At the beginning of this book, we noted that while the vast majority of the world population is self-identified as religious, religious practice has waned in some parts of the world. Heschel thinks such decline may be the fault of less than adequate religious practitioners who fail to live up to religion's call to a vibrant, loving faith.

"It is customary to blame secular science and anti-religious philosophy for the eclipse of religion in modern society. It would be more honest to blame religion for its own defeats. Religion declined not because it was refuted, but because it became irrelevant, dull, oppressive, insipid. When faith is completely replaced by creed, worship by discipline, love by habit; when the crisis of today is ignored because of the splendor of the past; when faith becomes an heirloom rather than a living fountain; when religion speaks only in the name of authority rather than with the voice of compassion–its message becomes meaningless."

Heschel's stress on the vital role of the celebration of faith should caution us in thinking that religious faith is always about a stern, unfeeling discipline. On this front, Heschel is commending the appeal to joy and awe reflected in Hebrew scriptures.

"People of our time are losing the power of celebration. Instead of celebrating we seek to be amused or entertained. Celebration is an active state, an act of expressing reverence or appreciation. To be entertained is a passive state–it is to receive pleasure afforded by an amusing act or a spectacle... Celebration is a confrontation, giving attention to the transcendent meaning of one's actions."

Heschel's more philosophical work brings together existential reflections on the human condition with analyses of classic texts like the biblical prophets. In Heschel's work one can see what was highlighted earlier: a spirituality that takes social justice seriously. Heschel's work is also extraordinary given his stress on celebration and joy, a truly life-affirming spirituality.

Christianity

Christians accept the Hebrew scriptures and Judaism's understanding of God's action in history. Christianity goes beyond Judaism, however, in holding that God became incarnate as Jesus of Nazareth whose birth, life, teaching, miracles, suffering, death, and resurrection are the principle means by which God delivers creation from its sin (moral and spiritual evil) and devastation. Jesus's teaching stressed an intimacy between himself and God as Father, as evident in the prayer he taught his disciples which weaves together praise, petition, and a call to forgiveness.

Our Father who art in heaven, hallowed be thy name.

Thy Kingdom come, Thy will be done
On earth as it is in heaven
Give us this day our daily bread
And forgive us our sins, as we forgive those
who sin against us
Lead us not into temptation, but deliver us
from evil
For thine is the Kingdom, the Power and
the Glory.

This is probably the most often recited religious prayer on earth, recited sometimes more than once a day in monasteries. Its beginning with addressing God as "Our Father" casts those offering this prayer as siblings, no matter what your age. If I am 90 years old, and you are 17, we are (from a God's eye point of view) brothers or sisters. The prayer has an existential edge in bidding one pray for *daily* bread, not praying for a yearly supply of bread (which, of course, is a symbol for all we need in terms of nourishment and material welfare). The petition for the forgiveness of sins does not allow the supplicants to ignore their neighbors; my forgiveness by God rests, in part, on whether I forgive those who have treated me unfairly.

The orthodox view that Jesus Christ ("Christ" meaning the anointed one) was fully God and fully human evolved over time. It may be plausibly argued that this high view of Christ (sometimes called *high Christology*) is found in the New Testament (especially in the context of the fourth of the four

Gospels, the Gospel according to John), but the explicit endorsement of a divine-human incarnation required a departure from Jewish monotheism and the development of a Trinitarian understanding of the Godhead.

The Trinity

As part of its teaching about the incarnation, Christianity holds that while God is one, God is constituted by three persons in a supreme, singular unity called the Trinity: Father, Son, and Holy Spirit. While some Christians have interpreted the Trinity as three modes or manifestations of God in human history (God appears as creator, redeemer, and sanctifier), the mainline tradition is that the inner life of God involves the three highest loves: each member of the Godhead has self-love, love of another (the Father loves the Son; the Son loves the Father, and so on), and the love of two for a third (the Father and the Son love the Holy Spirit, and so on). This interior, mutual indwelling of love constitutes the inner glory of God which then gives rise to God's overflowing loving creation and then redemption of the cosmos.

The Council of Chalcedon (451 CE), one of the seven ecumenical councils of early Christianity that established Christian orthodoxy, articulated the doctrine of the Incarnation in creedal form:

> We confess one and the same our Lord Jesus Christ… the same perfect in Godhead, the same in perfect manhood, truly God and truly man … acknowledged in two natures without confusion, without change, without division, without separation—the difference of natures being by no means taken away because of the union, but rather the distinctive character of each nature being preserved, and combining into one person and hypostasis—not divided or separated into two persons, but one and the same Son and only begotten God, Word, Lord Jesus Christ.

The doctrine can be stated even more concisely: In Jesus Christ, the Son of God –second person of the Trinity– took on human nature, thus becoming a unique individual person possessing two natures, one fully human and one fully divine. On this view, the Son became human by becoming embodied (feeling with a human body; acting, tasting, thinking, having appetites and all the senses as a human) and thus limited as a finite, incarnate being, while still remaining divine. It has been described as the two minds model of the incarnation, as when a person adopts and focuses on a limited mind-set or role – for example, someone may adopt the role of a college professor– while bracketing or not acting on their broader knowledge and power –the professor may be an uncle of one of his students but is so focused on treating the students equally he brackets or lays aside what he knows about his niece.

With the doctrine of the incarnation, Jesus is not identical to God in the logical sense of identity. Jesus is *totus deus* – wholly God – but not *totum dei* – the whole of God. For the fullness of the Godhead is Father, Son, and Holy Spirit, three persons conjoined in one nature.

Traditional Christianity asserts that through God's loving mercy and justice, individual persons are not annihilated at death, but either enjoy an afterlife of heaven or endure one of hell. Some Christians have been and are *universalists*, holding that ultimately God will triumph over all evil and there will be universal salvation for all people, though a greater part of the tradition holds that God will not violate the free will of creatures and that if persons seek to reject God, then those persons will be everlastingly separate from God.

Christians have advanced different accounts of how the life, teaching, death, and resurrection of Christ brings about an atonement (literally at-one-ment) between creatures and God. On one account, Christ takes on the punishment we deserve for our sins or wrongdoing; this is said to involve vicarious suffering, a case of when someone can take on the suffering of another person. On another account, Christ's saving power lies in his great manifestation of divine love – we are saved by imitating and learning from Christ's display of love. On still another account, Christ's atoning work lies in his providing us with eternal life whereby we may make-up or redeem the lives we have wasted (both our own and others). This later model sees Christ as addressing one factor we are hopeless of in terms of restoration. To take an extreme example, if you have murdered someone, you cannot bring them back to life, but God through Christ can. These and still other accounts can be complementary. Some Christians have held that an explicit trust in the saving power of Christ in this life is essential for salvation, while others have held that salvation through Christ may occur when persons seek out Christ-like virtues in this life or encounter Christ's saving power in life after death. Most Christians, over its two thousand year history, have held that death does not have the last word in terms of God's powerful, loving care.

Some unity of Christian belief and practice was gradually achieved in the course of developing various creeds (the word comes from the Latin *credo*, "I believe," with which the creeds used in worship traditionally began) that defined Christian faith in formal terms. The Nicene Creed, most of which was written and approved in the fourth century, is the most famous and most widely shared of these. At the heart of traditional Christianity is a ritual of initiation (baptism) and the eucharist, a rite that re-enacts or recalls Christ's self-offering through sharing blessed bread and wine (sometimes called *communion* or *mass*). What unity Christianity achieved was broken, however, in the eleventh century with the split between the Western (now the Roman Catholic Church) and Eastern, Byzantine Christianity (now the Orthodox Churches), and broken again in the sixteenth century with the split between the Catholic Church and the churches of the Reformation. Many denominations emerged after the Reformation, including the Anglican, Baptist, Lutheran, Methodist, and Presbyterian Churches. Since the middle of the twentieth century, greater unity between Christian communities has been pursued with some success. Some Christians treat the Bible as infallible and inerrant in its original form (free from error), while others treat the Bible as authoritative and inspired but not free from historical error or fallible human influence.

The most important early follower of Jesus was Paul the Apostle.

Paul's letters (referred to as *epistles*) make up the majority of the New Testament. We first meet Paul in the Book of Acts (a story of the early church) as a devout Jew who was persecuting Christians. He had no first-hand contact with Jesus's earthly life but encounters Jesus in a dramatic conversion experience while travelling on the road to Damascus. It is through the life and teaching of Paul that the early church sees itself as welcoming non-Jews or gentiles, and not demanding that converts to Christianity follow Jewish dietary laws and initiation through circumcision. One can see in Paul's writing the many factors that will contribute to what we might refer to as the Jesus movement becoming a major religion,

Christianity. Christianity grew through conversions in response to the apostolic proclamation of Jesus's resurrection and the fulfilling of prophecies, but also through martyrdom (Paul and others being put to death for their faith), creating a culture (or sub-culture) in which women had a higher, more respected role than in Greco-Roman culture, and providing a network of social care (dare we say love?) that enabled Christians to survive in greater numbers than the non-Christians or pagans of their time. In the second and third centuries, it is estimated that a fourth to a third of the population of the Roman Empire perished of plague (probably smallpox and measles). Some historians of Christianity propose that while 10% of Christians died of plague, 30% of non-Christians died as they lacked the network of care that Christian community provided. In the writings of Paul one can see him lay the groundwork for mutual care that would come into play after his own martyrdom sometime in the years 64-67 CE. His letters herald the primacy of grace, faith, and love over ritual purity and rigorous adherence to law. His missionary journeys to multiple cities in the Mediterranean basin is revealing in that Christianity was at the outset a largely urban movement and only gradually spread to rural parts of the Roman Empire.

While Paul is often thought of an intellectually-oriented Christian (in the Book of Acts he is pictured as debating non-Christian philosophers), in one of his letters in the New Testament we find this extraordinary stress on the indisputable primacy of love as even more important than faith.

> If I speak in the tongues of men or of angels, but do not have love, I am only a resounding gong or a clanging cymbal. 2 If I have the gift of prophecy and can fathom all mysteries and all knowledge, and if I have a faith that can move mountains, but do not have love, I am nothing. 3 If I give all I possess to the poor and give over my body to hardship that I may boast, but do not have love, I gain nothing.
>
> 4 Love is patient, love is kind. It does not envy, it does not boast, it is not proud. 5 It does not dishonor others, it is not self-seeking, it is not easily angered, it keeps no record of wrongs. 6 Love does not delight in evil but rejoices with the truth. 7 It always protects, always trusts, always hopes, always perseveres.
>
> 8 Love never fails. But where there are prophecies, they will cease; where there are tongues, they will be stilled; where there is knowledge, it will pass away. 9 For we know in part and we prophesy in part, 10 but when completeness comes, what is in part disappears. 11 When I was a child, I talked like a child, I thought like a child, I reasoned like a child. When I became a man, I put

the ways of childhood behind me. 12 For now we see only a reflection as in a mirror; then we shall see face to face. Now I know in part; then I shall know fully, even as I am fully known.

13 And now these three remain: faith, hope and love. But the greatest of these is love. (I Corinthians 13)

This praise of love supports the view that a loveless (or hate-filled) Christian faith is a contradiction in terms. In the theology of love in the early church, love of God and of neighbor are interwoven. It was taught that if one hates one's neighbor, a creature of God, you do not truly love God.

The early centuries of the Christian church included a myriad of teachers, priests, bishops, martyrs, and ordinary persons throughout the Roman Empire, but none were more influential than Augustine of Hippo (354-430). Augustine was born to a Christian mother (Monica) and non-Christian father in North Africa. He published the *Confessions*, an autobiography narrating his upbringing, education, intimate relations (he fathered a child), and the epic tale of his immersion in philosophy and religion until his conversion to Christianity when he was 31 years old. The book is remarkable for its interior, psychology, mixed with philosophical reflection on such awesome topics as the philosophy of time and space. His literary output was unprecedented in terms of published commentaries, sermons, treatises. Preeminent among his works is *The City of God* (composed between 413-426); it is a sweeping defense of Christianity and a portrait of history as a battle between God's kingdom and earthly paganism. The crucial event that led to this book was the sack of Rome in 410. Augustine replied to the charge that Christianity was to blame for the traumatic decline of the Empire.

There is not an area of Christianity that Augustine did not address – the sacraments, trinity, incarnation, free will and providence, and more. Perhaps his most extraordinary contribution was his treatment of the life of faith as a deeply personal, interior matter. He contended that living in light of God's presence involved an order of love (the *Ordo Amoris*). He called us to not get so caught up in external matters that we neglect the vast, important realm of our interior lives and loves. In *The Confessions*, Augustine writes:

> Men go abroad to wonder at the heights of mountains, at the huge waves of the sea, at the long courses of the rivers, at the vast compass of the ocean, at the circular motions of the stars, and they pass by themselves without wondering.

After Augustine, St. Anselm of Canterbury (1033-1109) was highly influential. Anselm was a Benedictine monk who was appointed as the Archbishop of Canterbury in 1093. He is famous for addressing the relationship between faith and reason. He developed what has come to be called "perfect being theology." From Anselm's perspective, God is maximally good, the supremely good reality who creates and sustains the cosmos through an overflowing of goodness. Anselm proposed that one may come to see that God is real by reflecting on the very nature of God's perfection. For readers with philosophical interests in his arguments, I recommend the entry "Philosophy of Religion" I wrote for the free online *Stanford Encyclopedia of Philosophy*. In this context I simply stress that, for Anselm, God's reality is (in a sense) simple in its being maximal; so, God does not have a limited amount of power and knowledge, but maximal power and knowledge. There is no equivalent in God of limits, such as (given the current laws of nature), a physical object cannot surpass the speed of light.

Anselm articulated and defended a view of the atonement according to which human sin creates a debt to God that cannot be repaid by humans except through the incarnation and the vicarious suffering of the perfect God-Man, Jesus Christ. According to Anselm, Jesus offered to God (the Father) a perfect sacrifice to atone for the sins of the world. Suffering on behalf of others may seem counter-intuitive (how can the suffering of an innocent person produce a merit that can alleviate the guilt of another?), but we can make sense of cases of self-offering or service that benefit others

– a person donates blood or their organs or pays the monetary debt of what someone else owes or when police, firefighters, soldiers give their lives in service to others. In the spirit of Anslem, some of these examples may fill out a portrait of how Jesus's life, sacrifice, and resurrection may be saving.

Augustine, Anselm, and Aquinas, taken together, are hard to overestimate in terms of their impact on the history of Christianity. Thomas Aquinas (1225–1274) shaped a great deal of subsequent Roman Catholic philosophy and theology. Born into an affluent family, Thomas became a Dominican monk, much to the displeasure of his family. He produced a colossal body of work that synthesized Christian faith with the philosophy of Aristotle. His understanding of nature, including human nature, animals and plants, virtue and vice, owes much to Aristotle. Thomas defended what will become known as natural theology; he proposed that we can gain some knowledge of God by reflection on nature without appealing to sacred revelation. While human reason can establish that there is a God, revelation is needed for us to know of the incarnation, the trinity, sacraments. His view that revelation complements our nature was articulated in terms of how divine grace (God's gracious revelation in the Bible) is said not to destroy or overshadow our nature, but to perfect it. Dante's impressive work, the *Divine Comedy*, may be read as embodying a Thomist framework. (As an aside, followers of Thomas are called Thomists, and he is sometimes just referred to as Aquinas; we get that name from his birthplace, the city Aquino.) In that fourteenth century poem, the pilgrim is lost until he is rescued by the figure of Virgil who may represent human, natural knowledge and power, who guides him through the Inferno and Purgatory. To get to Paradise, though, he needs to be led by the figure of Beatrice who may be read as embodying gracious revelation.

As we come to the sixteenth century, the unity of the Western Roman Catholic Church is broken by religious revolt. Martin Luther and John Calvin were at the forefront of this revolution.

Martin Luther (1483-1546) is best known for beginning a movement that would become the Reformation. It was Protestant (for the movement involved protesting the teaching and practices of the Roman Catholic Church). Luther was born to peasants in Eisleben, Germany, and joined an Augustinian monastery. As a young monk he was haunted by the idea that his inability to be perfect earned God's wrath and damnation. He studied at the university at Wittenberg where he became convinced that the church was corrupt, exploiting the poor, and for its teaching that one may be saved only through good works. He instead came to believe that we are saved by grace alone (faithful trust in the person and work of Christ). In 1517, Luther authored 95 Theses against the church's teachings and practices. The church excommunicated him in 1521. He lived for a time as an outlaw under the protection of German princes. He translated the Bible into German and came to teach that scripture alone (*sola scriptura*) was needed for the formation and life of faith; one did not need to rely on priests to mediate the truths of the Bible. Instead, he taught that all believers are akin to priests. Luther did not embrace Aquinas's natural theology, arguing that it was prideful and did not take seriously the devastating effects of the fall and sin. Luther was a fierce polemicist – arguing with little sympathy with his opponents. Much to the regret of subsequent Lutherans (as well as others), near the end of his life, Luther authored a fiercely anti-Semitic diatribe.

Luther is among the very few university professors to launch a religious movement. His standing up to ecclesiastical and state hierarchy has been heralded as a pivotal act of free speech. Luther sought to overcome the idea that there were special, sacred vocations, like being a priest, that were more holy than ordinary vocations like being a butcher or candlestick maker. God is sovereign and calls all persons to a life of dignity.

John Calvin (1509-1564) overlapped but outlived Martin Luther. He is sometimes thought of as leading the second generation of the Reformation. Born in France, he flourished in Geneva, Switzerland. Central to Calvin's teaching is that God is sovereign, just, and providential. Although controversial, Calvin seemed to allow natural theology a limited role (one may know *something* of God and the moral law without relying on the Bible), though like Luther he thought the effects of the fall leave us in a devastating state.

Although God offers a providential common grace whereby we humans may appreciate goodness and live humanely, our very being is depraved and we require the redeeming work of Christ to be saved. Calvinism is sometimes summarized by the abbreviation T.U.L.I.P. which stands for *total depravity*, *unconditional election* (God elects whom to save not based on merit), *limited atonement* (Christ's work atones for those who accept it, not for those who reject it), *irresistible grace* (if God elects to save you, you cannot resist it), and the *preservation of the saints* (once saved, you are always saved). While this theology may seem to us today to be quite unloving (it seems that, for Calvin, God may damn you to hell no matter what you do freely), but some subsequent Calvinists have drawn on the notion of God's irresistible and sovereign power to argue that God will (in the end) save all persons.

The Protestant movement was massive, but many Europeans remained faithful to the Roman Catholic Church, which launched what is known as the Counter-Reformation or the Catholic Reformation. This led to a widespread rejuvenation of Catholic faith and culture in Italy, central Europe, and the Iberian peninsula. I highlight here some important Spanish figures. Francisco de Vitoria (1483-1546) was a preeminent philosopher of law who was highly critical of the Spanish conquest of the Americas. He was one of the great contributors to the emergence of international law. As Europeans expanded their powers in terms of colonies and trade, it was Vitoria who sought to advocate on behalf of Native people. Known as "the father of international law," Vitoria defended a universal acceptance of all persons in terms of human dignity.

The Christian mystical tradition reached an apex in Spain, with profound impact today, in the life and work of the great Spanish mystics St. Theresa of Avila (1515-1582) and St. John of the Cross (1542-1591). As their fellow Spanish subjects navigated the globe, these two remarkable saints navigated the interior, spiritual quest to be unified with God. St. Theresa developed a spiritual inner life that overflowed in ecstatic rapture in the presence of Christ. A foremost Spanish poet, St. John wrote of the soul's journey to God through what he called "the dark night of the soul." To find God, one needs to pass through a purgation of the soul, being refined by virtue and faith.

Let us move ahead over two hundred years to the Danish Christian Soren Kierkegaard (1813-1855). He was a creative, eccentric, polemical existentialist who was highly critical of the established Lutheran church. The church had made Christianity seem routine and normal, whereas Kierkegaard saw Christian faith as shockingly radical, confronting us with what appears to be impossible. In one of his works, *Fear and Trembling*, he tells the story of Abraham and Isaac in terrifying terms, full of dread.

"It was early in the morning, Abraham arose betimes, he had the asses saddled, left his tent, and

Isaac with him, but Sarah looked out of the window after them until they had passed down the valley and she could see them no more. They rode in silence for three days. On the morning of the fourth day Abraham said never a word, but he lifted up his eyes and saw Mount Moriah afar off. He left the young men behind and went on alone with Isaac beside him up to the mountain... He stood still, he laid his hand upon the head of Isaac in benediction, and Isaac bowed to receive the blessing. And Abraham's face was fatherliness, his look was mild, his speech encouraging. But Isaac was unable to understand him, his soul could not be exalted; he embraced Abraham's knees, he fell at his feet imploringly, he begged for his young life, for the fair hope of his future, he called to mind the joy in Abraham's house, he called to mind the sorrow and loneliness. Then Abraham lifted up the boy, he walked with him by his side, and his talk was full of comfort and exhortation. But Isaac could not understand him. He climbed Mount Moriah, but Isaac understood him not. Then for an instant he turned away from him, and when Isaac again saw Abraham's face it was changed, his glance was wild, his form was horror."

Kierkegaard depicts Abrahamic faith as virtually incomprehensible from an outsider's point of view. Passionate obedience to God supersedes ethics. By re-telling the story of Abraham offering his son as a sacrifice in vivid, contemporary terms, Kierkegaard ruptured any notion that religious faith is a conventional, domestic affair. The life of faith is instead wild, brazen, even shocking.

Kierkegaard's body of written work was published under some pseudonyms, allowing him great versatility. He is regarded as an existentialist insofar as he focused on persons as individuals whose very being rests on their choices in the moment. He wrote a compelling treatise on love in which he praised the liberty of unrequited love. You may rightly love the love that comes from a spouse or friend, but if your primary object of love is their love, rather than they themselves, the following predicament can arise: if the spouse or friend ceases to love you for whatever reason, then the object of your love has ceased to be. Kierkegaard contended there is a greatness when a person continues their love of persons when that love is not returned.

Like Kierkegaard, the German Lutheran theologian Dietrich Bonhoeffer (1906-1945) held that conventional Christianity did not take seriously the cost of being a disciple of Jesus. He charged that Christians of his day did not appreciate the cost of God's grace; Christ gave his whole self for us and we are to give our whole selves to God's service. He is widely known for his taking an active part in the resistance movement to Adolf Hitler. He was imprisoned and executed just hours before the Allies would have liberated him. While in prison, he wrote poetry and letters, published in 1951 as *Letters and Papers from Prison*. Bonhoeffer stressed the vitality of personal encounter.

"The first service one owes to others in a community involves listening to them. Just as our love for God begins with listening to God's Word, the beginning of love for others is learning to listen to them. God's love for us is shown by the fact that God not only gives God's Word but also lends us God's ear [...] We do God's work for our brothers and sisters when we learn to listen to them."

In what remains of this section, "Christianity," let us briefly consider Christianity from an Afro-American perspective in terms of social justice.

Martin Luther King, Jr. (1929-1968) was an Afro-American civil rights activist and Baptist minister. King drew upon his Christian faith and the teachings of Mahatma Gandhi to lead a movement of nonviolent resistance on behalf of the civil rights of African Americans in the United States. His famous "Letter from Birmingham Jail" (1963) criticized white pastors. King advanced a theology of radical love to confront the hatred of racism. He was a man of intelligence and action. "The ultimate measure of a man is not where he stands in moments of comfort and convenience, but where he stands at times of challenge and controversy."

King helped prepare the way for a Black liberation theology. One of the prominent leaders of Black theology was James Cone (1938-2018). A professor at Union Theological Seminary in New York City, Cone critiqued the hypocrisy and racism among white Christians and sought to promote the vibrancy of Black culture borne out of suffering and struggle against white supremacy. Cone's theology drew on Afro-American folktales, poetry, psalms and the experience in Black churches, which functioned as a refuge, counter to a monolithic white culture.

"Black churches are very powerful forces in the African American community and always have been. Because religion has been that one place where you have an imagination that no one can control. And so, as long as you know that you are a human being and nobody can take that away from you, then God is that reality in your life that enables you to know that."

Cone wrote a groundbreaking book, *Black Theology & Black Power* in 1969, that was highly influential.

Islam

The Prophet Muhammad (570-632) is believed to be a descendent of Abraham through his firstborn Ishmael. He proclaimed a radical monotheism that explicitly repudiates the Christian teaching about the trinity. There are over 90 verses in the Qur'an that refer to Jesus, who is praised as a prophet sent from God / Allah.

"O People of the Book! Commit no excesses in your religion: Nor say of Allah aught but the truth. Christ Jesus the son of Mary was (no more than) a messenger of Allah, and His Word, which He bestowed on Mary, and a spirit proceeding from Him: so believe in Allah and His messengers. Say not "Trinity": desist: it will be better for you: for Allah is one Allah: Glory be to Him: (far exalted is He) above having a son. To Him belong all things in the heavens and on earth."

The Qur'an (from the Arabic for "to recite" or "to read"), its holy book, was, according to tradition, received by Mohammed, who dictated this revelation of Allah revealed to him by the Archangel Gabriel and is taken to be God's very speech. Central to Islam is the sovereignty of Allah, his providential control of the cosmos, the importance of living justly and compassionately, and of following a set practice of prayer, worship, and pilgrimage.

The Five Pillars of Islam are reciting the Islamic creed, praying five times a day while facing Mecca, alms-giving, fasting during Ramadan (the ninth month of the Muslim calendar), and making a pilgrimage to Mecca. In addition to the Qur'an, the Hadith is regarded as an important source of wisdom and teaching. Defined as speech, account, or narrative, "hadith" refers to what the Prophet Muhammad said or did. Hadiths were compiled by the Prophet's companions, the generation of Muslims who lived with the Prophet, and were transmitted orally before being written down and compiled decades or even centuries later. Hadiths are second in authority only to the Qur'an and comprise the Sunna, the standards and practices approved by the Prophet and thus used to guide standards and practices for Muslims through Islamic Law. One of my favorite hadith passages is about trusting Allah but exercising practical care. "Anas ibn Malik reported: A man said, "O Messenger of Allah, should I tie my camel and trust in Allah, or should I leave her untied and trust in Allah?" The Prophet, peace and blessings be upon him, said, 'Tie her and trust in Allah.'"

The two greatest branches of Islam are the Sunnis and Shi'ites, which developed early in the history of Islam over a disagreement about who would succeed Mohammed. Sunnis comprise a vast majority of Muslims. Shi'ites put greater stress on the continuing revelation of God beyond the Qur'an as revealed in the authoritative teachings of the *imam* (holy successors who inherit Mohammed's "spiritual abilities"), the *mujtahidun* ("doctors of the law"), and other agents. Sunnis succeeded in the early years of Islam, as the first three Caliphs were not blood relations to the Prophet. In the Battle of Karbala (680 CE), Sunni forces overwhelmed the Shiites. Since then, the Sunnis have been the dominant form of Islam in the Middle East and the world. Shiites make up about 15% of Muslims worldwide, mostly in Iran, with significant numbers in Azerbaijan (more than 80% of the population), Iraq (almost 65%), Lebanon, Yemen, and elsewhere.

Sufism is a smaller sub-set of Muslims who engage in mystical rites and meditation. They have sometimes been shunned by the overall Islamic community because of some Sufi mystics claiming to have achieved union with Allah. Sufis stress the immanence of God and the possibility of experiencing God here and now. Sufism is a method for bringing one into union or communion with God. The Sufi experience of divine union led to a deep and profound understanding of God and union with the divine that was inaccessible to and beyond the comprehension of those approaching Islam utilizing a purely theoretical approach. Sufis strive to always be aware of the presence of God, and they emphasize contemplation over the academic exercise of analytical reflection, and spiritual intimacy over jurisprudence and legalism. It utilizes such ritual practices as the recitation of prayers, meditation on passages in the Qur'an, and religious poetry. Emphasizing the role of the imagination and emotion in worship, Sufis use such terms as joy, ecstasy, and spiritual intoxication to describe their encounters with the divine. But they also use the term sobriety, which is the condition one comes to after having come out of the intoxicated ecstasy of union. Both intoxication and sobriety are important dimensions of Sufi teaching and experience. A great Sufi poet (to be addressed below), Rumi, puts in succinct terms the Sufi notion that one can find true love and joy from within:

> There is a candle in your heart, ready to be kindled.
> There is a void in your soul, ready to be filled.
> You feel it, don't you?"

Sufis believe that one needs to renounce worldly greed, seek inner purification, and then find insight and illumination from within.

Like Christianity, Islam has proclaimed that a loving, merciful, and just God will not annihilate an individual at death, but provide either heaven or hell. It may seem odd to think of hell positively, but some argue that justice demands that wickedness be punished or in some fashion defeated. It has also been argued that to believe a person's choices in this life can have eternal consequences reflects a very high view of the importance of our lives here and now. In Islam, as well as Judaism, divine forgiveness is predicated on repentance but not on the mediation of an atoning savior.

Unfortunately, in the West, Islam is often viewed with suspicion by non-Islamic peoples, largely due to great attention in the media on the Islamic State and highly conservative, rogue Muslim sects such as Wahhabism in Saudi Arabi that ferment violence and harsh applications of Islamic law or Sharia. No doubt there has been deeply regrettable violence done in the name of Islam, but we do well to remember when violence has been done in the past and today in the name of Christianity. A small point about vocabulary: the term "Jihad" means "struggle" and not holy warfare. In fact, Muhammad himself thought that the great jihad was the inner, personal, spiritual struggle to turn away from sin and to live righteously. (A parenthetic note to readers who struggle with writing; working on your writing has been called "the jihad of the pen"!) The great Islamic philosopher Al-Ghazali makes clear that "jihad" is not an exclusively military term: "Declare your jihad on thirteen enemies you cannot see – Egoism, Arrogance, Conceit, Selfishness, Greed, Lust, Intolerance, Anger, Lying, Cheating, Gossiping and Slandering. If you can master and destroy them, then you will be ready to fight the enemy you can see."

The impression of violence is exacerbated by the many anti-Muslim websites that cherry-pick qur'anic verses which, pulled out of context, seem to support violence. Consider the so-called 'Sword Verse,' the fifth verse of the ninth sura: "Fight and slay the Pagans wherever you find them, and seize them, beleaguer them, and lie in wait for them in every stratagem." Anti-Muslims (and, sadly, some Islamic terrorists) take this passage to be supporting violence against anyone who qualifies in their view as being a Pagan or non-believer. This is a most unfortunate interpretation. Utilizing similar hermeneutical contortions, one could use the Bible or any number of sacred or non-sacred texts to support violence against the innocent.

Let's examine the verse in context. The full verse reads, "But when the forbidden months are past, then fight and slay the Pagans wherever you find them, and seize them, beleaguer them, and lie in wait for them in every stratagem (of war); but if they repent, and establish regular prayers and practice regular charity, then open the way for them: for Allah is Oft-forgiving, Most Merciful." This sura or chapter is addressing the question of how to respond to an enemy when that enemy has violated a treaty that has been agreed upon by both parties. The chapter teaches that there should be a pause of several months to permit penitence and reconciliation before responding. If that does not occur, then war is allowed. Yet it also adds that if the offending party does repent and so forth, then "open the way for them." This passage has nothing to do with attacking innocent individuals or with advocating war against those who desire to coexist in peace and harmony. This is only one example, but a little research will demonstrate that the same general principle applies, if allowed a charitable read, to each of those qur'anic passages that are misinterpreted by some as texts of violence and terror.

Sadly, there are those who have hijacked Islam for their own political and perverse ends and attempt to force conversion to their own narrow views. But the Qur'an unequivocally states, "Let there be no compulsion in religion" (2:256) and "So if they dispute with you, say 'I have submitted my whole self to Allah, and so have those who follow me.' And say to the People of the Scripture and to the unlearned: 'Do you also submit yourselves?' If they do, then they are on right guidance. But if they turn away, your duty is only to convey the Message. And in Allah's sight are all of His servants." (3:20)

Islam and Peace

The son-in-law of Muhammad, Ali, was explicit in promoting the protection of non-Muslims. Ali is known for bearing many titles such as Lion of God, the God-fearer, the Prince of Faith. He was much admired for his bravery by Gandhi and Nelson Mandela. He should be known, too, for his promotion of tolerance and friendship.

"Hazrat Ali says that as a caliph and a ruler, he promises safety and security of life, property, honor, social status and religious freedom to non-Muslims and they should not be maltreated and looked down upon. So long as they do not try to betray and injure the cause of the state of Islam they should not be molested and should be allowed to practice their religion and trades freely and openly. Islam teaches us to carry a message of peace with us and improve the status of society wherever we go and the best way to achieve this is to create amity, friendliness and concord amongst human beings. Therefore, Muslims should try to develop friendship of these people and should never resort to wrong use of power, force or arrogance."

Al-Kindi (c.813-873), Al-Farabi (c.870-950), Avicenna (980-1037), and Averroes (1126-1198) are among the four most famous Muslim philosophers who promoted natural theology and accounts of nature and virtue that synthesized Aristotle's work with the teachings of the Qur'an. These philosophers had a formidable challenge from Al-Ghazali, who accused the philosophers of straying from orthodox Islam, which should treat the Qur'an as a supreme authority over secular philosophy. In his autobiography, *Deliverance from Error*, he recounts how philosophy led him to a state of despair until, after a protracted time of renunciation and seclusion, he had a transformative mystical awakening. Al-Ghazali stressed the centrality of grace, God, as the absolute creator of the cosmos from nothing, and God's causal role in the sustaining of all of creation.

The eighth to the thirteenth century has been called the Golden Age of Islam. There was an abundance of scholarship, science, mathematics. The epicenter of intellectual activity was Baghdad, which hosted the House of Wisdom, one of the greatest libraries at the time. Islam expanded very rapidly from the Arabian peninsula throughout the middle east, Asia, Africa, the great islands in the Mediterranean, India, the Iberian peninsula, parts of southern Italy. Islamic expansion and culture became seriously compromised by Mongol invasion. Tragically, the House of Wisdom was destroyed during the siege of Baghdad in 1258 by Mongol forces.

Islam recovered from the Mongol attacks, and expanded dramatically. The fall of Constantinople in 1453 marked the end of the Christian Byzantine Empire.

I believe readers will appreciate taking note of a Muslim poet, mentioned briefly above, who is much loved around the world today. Rumi (1207-1273) was born in what is now the modern country of Afghanistan. As a young man he traveled widely in Persia and Arabia, settling in the city of Konya in what is now central Turkey where he was a professor of modern sciences. An encounter with a Sufi master when Rumi was 37 years old led him to give himself over to a life of mysticism and poetry. His poetic vision of life before God (one might even say life within God) involves a profound love of life itself.

Here is a Rumi poem, *Out There You'll Find*, that speaks to our finding richness within, without getting tied up in external relations.

Out there you'll find
dead souls
strange crowds
from East and West
a voice calls you to
follow the source
look inside
and you'll find
a human sea.

This vision is in concert with Augustine's notion of the importance of not getting so caught up in the external world that one neglects the almost boundless world within.

Rumi's poetry covers multiple topics, romance and eros, the love between the soul and God, wisdom, transformation, the seasons, women, and more. He is suspicious of rationalism, and praises instead passionate love.

> Love is reckless; not reason.
> Reason seeks a profit.
> Love comes on strong,
> consuming herself, unabashed.
> Yet, in the midst of suffering,
> Love proceeds like a millstone,
> hard surfaced and straightforward.
> Having died of self-interest,
> she risks everything and asks for nothing.
> Love gambles away every gift God bestows.
> Without cause God gave us Being;
> without cause, give it back again.

Rumi's praise of reckless love may be read as an antidote to the rationalistic dimension of Islamic philosophy that flourished in Baghdad and other centers of learning. The spirit of Islam may best be encountered when reading Rumi along with the rationalist Muslim philosopher al-Kindi.

Rumi's poetry today sells around the globe in the millions to people of all faiths as well as to those without religious affiliation. True to his capacious appeal, when he died in Konya in 1273, Jews and Christians joined Muslims in honoring him.

Given the importance of highlighting Muslims who stand for peace, consider a twentieth century

Iranian Muslim, Morteza Motahhari (1919-1979), a Shia cleric and philosopher. He was a superb philosopher who was highly supportive of the sciences while insisting that the sciences themselves are insufficient in explaining the very existence of the cosmos in which science is practiced. I reference him here, however, for another quality of this great man. He was active in the 1979 Iranian revolution and very close to the top leadership. At the time, Iranian Marxists launched a campaign to hijack the revolution, turning it Marxist. Motahhari could easily have silenced, even imprisoned them, but he did not. Instead, he chose to reply to their case for Iranian Marxism with arguments. In other words, he chose the path of nonviolence. He paid for this with his life as the Marxists had him assassinated. I suggest he was not just a martyr (or shahid) on behalf of the establishment of the Islamic Republic of Iran but to the nonviolent pursuit of the love of wisdom for the sake of religious faith.

Abrahamic Faiths in Global Perspective

Do observant Jews, Christians, and Muslims worship the same God? While reasonable persons may answer this differently, there is some reason to think the answer is 'yes' given their historical rootedness in Abrahamic faith. While Judaism and Islam explicitly repudiate the Christian notion of God's triune nature, traditional Christians have held that the tri-personal nature of God is not tri-theism (or polytheism) but compatible with monotheism (the oneness of God's nature). While the Christian idea of the incarnation is in tension (if not outright contradiction) to Judaism and Islam, Judaism has historically adhered to something analogous to an incarnation in its teaching that God becomes manifest in this life as wisdom and the Qur'an itself functions as a manifestation in this life of the eternal Word of God.

While Judaism is an ethnic religion, Christianity and Islam are not. Christianity and Islam have spread through missionary work, migration, and to some extent through conquest and imperial or state expansion. Although in the popular mind it may be thought that the majority of Muslims are Arabs, this is not the case; over 60% of Muslims are in Southeast Asia. One reason for the appeal of Christianity and Islam is that they seem to crystalize or provide unified worldviews for persons drawn to a unified, theistic worldview with sustaining rites and sacred texts. So, some of the success in the spread of Christianity and Islam throughout the African continent is that the indigenous pre-Christian and pre-Islamic culture often reflected the belief in a supreme, all powerful, all knowing God, as supported by oral tradition and sages. Christians and Muslims sought to present themselves as fulfilling or giving shape to what Africans already upheld.

Each of the Abrahamic faiths has had to struggle with rival alternatives. There have been deeply painful times when observant Jews have been given the alternative of converting to Christianity or suffer expulsion, as in Spain in the late fifteenth century, along with a host of persecutions cited earlier. At the outset, Christianity struggled with a first century movement referred to as Gnosticism. This movement had various forms, but in general Gnostics saw this world as corrupt and the creation of a wicked or imperfect power. They instead looked to the God beyond this world-creator for liberation from the material world. Gnostics who professed to be Christians resisted the notion that God would become fully incarnate (mingling the perfect divine nature with vile matter). Christian tradition itself resisted this low view of the material, created world. At its inception, Islam had to struggle against the polytheism on the Arabian peninsula and to face down one of the largest religions in the middle east (especially Iran) and in the world at the time, Zoroastrianism. This tradition began around 1000 BCE (though some scholars propose it may date back to the second millennium BCE), with its powerful vision of the cosmos being contested by two, rival spirits, the good Ahura Mazda and the evil Ahriman. Ultimately, Islam vanquished Zoroastrianism, though there are estimates of there still being around 150,000 practicing Zoroastrians today.

Of course the most famous military clash between Christianity and Islam were the series of crusades that began in 1095 and concluded by 1291. Historians estimate that the crusades involved around a million deaths. The typical textbook outlook casts the crusades in terms of European Christians aggressively seeking land and wealth from Muslim lands. The truth is a bit more mixed: for whatever motivated Pope Urban II to launch the first crusade, it should be appreciated that, prior to the crusades, Muslim armies had conquered Persia and vast land that had Christian communities: Syria, Egypt, northern Africa, most of Spain, southern Italy, and major islands including Cyprus, Rhodes, Sardinia, Majorca, and Crete. There was intense, fierce fighting on both sides. But let's end on a brighter note about a great Muslim warrior who rescued Christians from tremendous violence.

At great risk to himself and his family, the Muslim warrior Abd al-Qadir (1808-1883) rescued up to 100,000 US and European diplomats, merchants and their families, priests and nuns in the riots of Damascus, Syria, in July of 1860. Al-Qadir was the past leader of the resistance to the French occupation of Algeria, his homeland, who conducted his campaigns with an extraordinary reputation of dignity and chivalry. After his capture by the French and release to Damascus, he and his sons protected his former enemies, the French, with such bravery that the French awarded him the Legion of Honor, along with an annual pension. In today's toxic anti-

Muslim climate, it would be good to recall that Americans used to acknowledge this great man: he even had a town named after him in Iowa, Elkader. He received gifts not only from Queen Victoria and other European heads of state, but also from the most outstanding Republican President of the United Sates, Abraham Lincoln.

Before moving to religions from Asia, let us consider three questions that some readers are likely to have. Are the Abrahamic faiths still viable intellectually today? From the standpoint of the Abrahamic faiths, what is the relationship between God and ethics? How might these faiths respond to the problem of evil?

So, what are the prospects of theism today? Some popular writers ridicule the God of Abrahamic faith as a kind of aberration, a giant poltergeist or teacup or Spaghetti Monster. Such caricatures may amuse but they should not avert our gaze from some astounding facts: there seems no necessity of our cosmos coming into existence and continuing to exist. Why is there a cosmos with uniform laws of nature enabling there to be stars and planets, galaxies and at least on our planet (and probably many more) life, including conscious beings (human and nonhuman) in which there has emerged ethical practices, religious traditions in which persons report what appears to them to be experiences of the divine, and the sciences? The natural sciences can indeed explain many things about the cosmos (biological evolution can account for the emergence and diversification of life) but not about why there is a cosmos at all in which physics and chemistry are constant. Theism can offer an account in terms of the purposive, powerful, creative conservation of God, whose necessary existence means God is self-sufficient and not dependent on any other being or force. Those denying theism, like the philosopher Bertrand Russell, maintain that "the cosmos just is" without any cause or explanation. I suggest that is not entirely reasonable: if everything in the cosmos has an explanation (or cause), why should we not seek out the explanation of the cosmos as a whole?

What is the relationship between God and ethics in the Abrahamic faiths? There are a growing number of books with titles like "Good without God" or "Morality without God." Why think that the existence of God makes any difference to ethics? To our understanding of value? In fact, don't we need a standard of value that is independent of God in order to recognize God as good or recognizing that a divine command is authoritative? Some Christian philosophers like Immanuel Kant have claimed that divine commands can only reinforce what we already know to be right or wrong.

I suggest that there are some bad and some good reasons for thinking that the existence or non-existence of God matters a great deal for everything, including ethics. A bad reason would be to think that ethics can only be valid if backed up by an omnipotent being who will give rewards to those God favors (or do as they are told) and punish those who do not do what God commands. Another reason that seems weak is to claim that one must believe in an all-good, all-powerful God if one is going to lead a good life. It seems even weaker to hold that no one would know anything about good or evil, right or wrong, without the Bible or the Qur'an.

For the sake of argument, let's assume (as most of us actually believe) that secular atheists and agnostics (or, more generally, those who do not believe in an all-powerful, all-good God) can be just, compassionate, courageous, respectful, courageous, and so on. Let us also assume that if God exists in accordance with the Abrahamic religions, God is not worthy of worship and obedience solely on the basis of God's power. In such a theology of power, God would be like an omnipotent Caesar. Rather, the important and relevant matter is whether the fact (if it is one) that we are part of a creation that is sustained by an all-good, omnipresent God who has made us for the good and calls all persons to a life of goodness (i.e. justice, compassion, etc.) that would include relations between persons and all creatures in the cosmos and communion with the Creator (and, if Christianity is right, in communion with the redeemer Jesus Christ) makes a vital difference to the meaning of our lives, including our ethics. I suggest that the answer is a clear "yes!" If true, this would mean that reality is far more immense in time and space and value than we ordinarily assume. It would mean that wrongful acts are not only wrong because of the harm to a person (for example) but harm to a person who is loved by God and created for the good. It also would mean that there are resources to draw on for the good that can be added to the resources available in a secular worldview. Consider the charge that was made by Albert Camus, the great atheistic existentialist about what we must do (ideally):

"We must mend what has been torn apart, make justice imaginable again in a world so obviously unjust, give happiness a meaning once more to peoples poisoned by the misery of the century. Naturally, it is a superhuman task. But superhuman is the term for tasks that take a long time to accomplish, that's all."

If the God of Abrahamic faith exists, then we are not alone in setting out to do justice and bring happiness into the lives of peoples who have been otherwise poisoned by hate or are the victims of hate.

If the God of Abrahamic tradition exists, why is there any evil at all? Or, if some evil is understandable, why so much evil? In general, the Abrahamic faiths treat goodness as more primordial than evil. That is, evil is often seen as the impairing or damaging of something good. It is evil to kill an innocent person because it is good that there are innocent persons. Most things that are good, however, are good for their own sake and not because they impair or damage something evil. The health of a person seems to be a positive good; it is not just the absence of disease. The common conviction in Judaism, Christianity, and Islam that the cosmos was created good inclines believers to hold that cruelty, murder, rape, oppression each involves a dysfunction or impairment of something that should be good. When persons are cruel, murderous, rapists, oppressors they are misusing their minds and bodies that God has purposed for them to use to promote compassion, life, dignity and respect, justice. So, the Abrahamic traditions differ radically from the standpoint of secular naturalism. From such a standpoint (especially when accompanied by a belief that all is determined by the laws of nature) evil is natural; cruelty, murder, rape, and oppression are inevitable parts of the natural world. The Abrahamic faiths, on the other hand, see such evil as an aberration, something abhorrent to God / Allah, each rape is a case of sacrilege, an abomination. So, why doesn't God destroy all evil and all evil-doers? Or prevent any evil at all from coming into creation?

I cannot hope to fully address such a question here. But I can report that theists have made many replies. One is called 'the greater good defense,' according to which there are great goods in there being a stable cosmos with laws of nature and persons who have free will and are responsible for each other's care. In such a world, God has to grant some autonomy to persons and the cosmos, not miraculously interfering whenever someone sets out to do something evil. Some philosophers distinguish the ethics of creation (what kind of cosmos might a good God bring into being and sustain?) and the ethics within creation (what are the kinds of acts good persons should do in creation?). Concerning the later, you and I should intervene and prevent cruelty when we can (unless doing so would create greater cruelty). Concerning the ethics of creation, however, our perspective needs to broaden. Here is a broad picture of creation from a broadly Abrahamic perspective without including factors that are specific to only one of the traditions (so, there is no inclusion of the incarnation).

There is an omnipotent, omniscient, all-good God of perfect love who has created and sustains a cosmos of at least one hundred billion galaxies in which there are (perhaps uncountably) many planets, at least one of which sustains life (there may or not be others—perhaps many billions of others). All the elements of the cosmos, with their causal powers and liabilities, are dependent upon divine creation and conservation such that none of them would endure over time without God's causal powers. The cosmos appears to be marked by uniform, stable laws that we currently are discovering through physics, chemistry, and biology. The vastness and grandeur of this cosmos merits our awe and delight as something sublime and of extraordinary beauty. On earth, chemical bonding led to the emergence of life and through a long, complex evolutionary history, there has emerged plant and animal life, the biota and abiota. Amid the multitude of nonhuman animal life, some developed and are developing powers of movement and sentience, and with some mammals, including humans, there emerges persons (selves or subjects) who have powers of movement, a range of senses and feelings, memory, reason, the power to love or hate, fear and desire, and (eventually) powers to make moral judgments and to act in light of what seem to be right or wrong choices, in accordance with virtues and vices. Some use these powers for the good and welfare of persons and other forms of life, which are beautiful ends, but some use their powers for profoundly ugly and wrong ends. In this cosmos, there are good and beautiful friendships, families, adventures, creativity, and there are evil and ugly enemies, hateful rulers, and soul-destroying acts such as rape, torture, murder, enslavement. These evils are contrary to the will and nature of God, abhorrent to God's purpose in creation. The cosmos contains abundant goods, but also earthquakes, floods, droughts, diseases, wildfires, plagues. The damage caused is sometimes increased or decreased due to human factors, but sometime calamities occur unaffected by human action and inaction. God acts through prophets and other created agents to fight and prevent some evils, but not always. Thus, while God commands persons not to murder, and judges each murderer guilty of a heinous crime and sacrilege, God does not miraculously intervene to prevent every murder. God seeks to be revealed and in relationship with created persons through experiences and events, through prophets and sages. Ultimately, God enters the created order through prophets (such as Moses, Jesus, Muhammad) who teach about the goodness and love of God, justice and mercy. God / Allah will sustain persons at death in order to offer an opportunity of redemption beyond this life.

What do you think of the above picture of the cosmos? Do we know that this is impossible? Some do make such a claim. They may then adopt atheism or adjust some of the premises, proposing that God may not be perfectly good or loving or may not be omnipotent or omniscient. God, as conceived of by Aristotle, was not omnipotent nor omniscient. But claiming to know the above is impossible is a tall order. Are our human faculties so developed that we can reliably reach such a confident conclusion? Also, the implications of believing that our cosmos is so evil that it is unworthy of being created by a good God may have some practical consequences that are controversial (e.g. anti-natalists today argue that the world is so bad, it is wrong to procreate and to bring children into such a world). A more qualified response would be that the above seems to you unlikely or, even more qualified, an agnostic response (I do not know it is impossible or unlikely and I also do not know it is possible and likely). Interestingly, some philosophers adopt a position they call skeptical theism, according to which it is reasonable to believe in an all-good God but not reasonable to believe that one can "solve" the problem of evil. Other positions: one may claim either to know the above Abrahamic worldview is true or to have faith that it is true. Faith does not require knowledge. Nor does hope. You may hope that there is an all-powerful, loving God that can bring good out of evil without knowing this is the case.

There is a double question in a Latin phrase worth pondering: *Si Deus est, unde malum? Si non est, unde bonum?* If there is a God, why is there evil? If there is not, why is there good?

Let us now turn our immersion to the East.

Chapter 3

Hinduism, Buddhism, and Jainism in India; Confucianism and Daoism in China

While Judaism, Christianity, and Islam originated in the Near East, the other major world religions, Hinduism, Buddhism, Jainism, Confucianism, and Daoism, originated in India and China.

A minor point about terminology: While I noted earlier the importance of avoiding stereotypes about Western versus Eastern philosophies, it is still possible to refer to the religions in this chapter as "Eastern" in terms of their origin, but the term "Asian" is a bit more problematic. In English "Asia" is a reasonably well-defined but broad geographical term, designating everything from the Bosporus to the Bering Straits, from Siberia to Sri Lanka. This expanse includes West

Asia, where the three "Western" monotheisms arose, as well as the Iranian world, South and Southeast Asia, China and East Asia, North and Central Asia. Attempts to encapsulate the languages, literatures, religions, philosophies, theologies throughout the very diverse cultural areas concerned are inevitably problematic and for this reason I will sometimes refer to what is Eastern (in origin) or, more specifically, refer to India and China.

Hinduism

Hinduism is so diverse that it is difficult to use the term as an umbrella category even to designate a host of interconnected ideas and traditions. "Hindu" is Persian for "Indian" and was introduced to name the various traditions that have flourished in the Indian subcontinent, going back to before the second millennium BCE. The most common feature of what is considered Hinduism is reverence for the Vedic scriptures, a rich collection of work, some of it highly philosophical, especially the *Upanishads* (written between 800 and 500 BCE). Unlike the three monotheistic religions, Hinduism does not look back to a singular (ostensible) historical figure such as Abraham, Jesus, or Muhammad.

According to one strand of Hinduism, Advaita Vedanta (a strand that has received a great deal of attention from Western philosophers in this and the last century), this world of space and time is ultimately illusory. The world is *Maya* (literally "illusion"). The world appears to us to consist of diverse objects because we are in ignorance. Behind the diverse objects and forms we observe in what may be called the phenomenal or apparent world (the world of phenomena and appearances) there is the formless, impersonal reality of Brahman, and this school's principal aim is the rejection of this duality ("Advaita" comes from the Sanskrit term for "non-duality").

Brahman alone is ultimately real. This position is often called *monism* (from the Greek *monus* or "single") or *pantheism* ("God is everything"). Shankara (also spelled Sankara, Samkara, or Sankaracharya) (788–820) was one of the greatest teachers of this monist, nondualist tradition within Hinduism. In his *Crest-Jewel of Discrimination* he explained that "Brahman alone is real. There is none but He. When He is known as the supreme reality there is no other existence but Brahman." "In dream," he wrote in the same book, "the mind creates by its own power a complete universe of subject and object. The waking state [too] is only a prolonged dream. The phenomenal universe exists in the mind."

Other theistic strands of Hinduism construe the Divine as personal, all-good, powerful, knowing, creative, loving, and so on. Theistic elements may be seen, for example, in the *Bhagavad Gita* and its teaching about the love of God. Some of the breathtaking passages about Krishna's divine manifestation even seem similar to the great passages in the Gospel of John, when Christ proclaims or implies his divinity or divine calling. Madhva (thirteenth and fourteenth centuries) is one of the better known theistic representatives of Hinduism.

There are also lively polytheistic elements within Hinduism. Popular Hinduism has been called the religion of 330 million gods. The recognition and honor paid to these gods are sometimes absorbed into Brahman worship, as the gods are understood to be so many manifestations of the one true reality.

Whether theirs is the monist or the theistic form, many Hindus believe that a trinity of Brahma, Vishnu, and Shiva is the cardinal, supreme manifestation of Brahman. Brahma is the creator of the world, Vishnu its sustainer, manifested in the world as Krishna and Rama, incarnations or avatars (from the Sanskrit for "one who descends") who instruct and enlighten, and Shiva the destroyer.

Most Hindus believe in reincarnation. The soul migrates through different lives, according to principles of *karma* (Sanskrit for "deed" or "action"), the moral consequence of one's actions. The final consummation or enlightenment is *moksha* (or release) from *samsara*, the material cycle of birth and rebirth. In the monist forms, liberation comes from overcoming the dualism of Brahman and the individual self or soul (*atman*, "breath"), and sometimes from merging into a transcendental self with which all other selves are identical.

Karma is often associated with (and believed to be a chief justification for) a strict social caste system. Not all Hindus support such a system, and many Hindu reformers in the modern era argue for its abolition. One of the well-known reform movements is the Arya Samaj, founded by Swami Dananda Saraswati (1824–83).

Hindu Inclusivity

Hinduism has a legacy of inclusive spirituality. It understands other religions as different ways to enlightened unity with Brahman. In the *Bhagavad Gita*, Krishna declares:

> If any worshipper do reverence with
> faith to any God whatever,
> I make his faith firm,
> and in that faith he reverences his
> god,
> and gains his desires,
> for it is I who bestow them. (vii. 21–2)

Hinduism has also absorbed and, to some extent, integrated some of the teaching and narratives of Buddhism. It has also assimilated Christian elements, especially since British colonialism, with

Jesus being seen as the tenth avatar of Vishnu. Although Hinduism and Islam have sometimes been in painful conflict, there are cases of tolerance and collaboration. One of the aims of Sikhism, a sixteenth century reform movement within Hinduism, was to bring together Hindus and Muslims (to be addressed in chapter four).

For the rest of this section on Hinduism, let us take a snapshot look at Krishna, yoga, Bhakti, and Gandhi.

Krishna, whose name in Sanskrit means "the all attractive," the eighth avatar of Vishnu or the supreme God, is widely celebrated and worshipped throughout Hindu tradition. He is recognized as a God of love, wisdom, tenderness, and compassion. In addition to being the charioteer instructing Arjuna in wisdom, he is sometimes pictured as a divine hero, a lover (surrounded by adoring women), a prankster, a cow herder, or a god-child. He has been portrayed in dramatic terms aiding those in distress. He is imaged as having black-blue skin, dancing, playing the flute, wearing a crown and clothed in yellow. From a theological point of view he has been construed (or interpreted) as conveying either a monistic or theistic model of the divine. In the Upanishad, there is a mantra invoking Krishna by his name and by the name "Rama" which means "He who is the reservoir of all pleasure." "Hare" refers to the inconceivable potency. Recitation of the mantra is often construed as freeing one's mind from earthly care.

Hare Rama Hare Rama
Rama Rama Hare Hare
Hare Krishna Hare Krishna
Krishna Krishna Hare Hare

The International Society for Krishna Consciousness was founded in the 1960s to promote Bhakti yoga.

The term 'yoga' is from the Sanskrit meaning "yoking" or "harnessing" of one's mind and body. In Hindu philosophy, Yoga is one of six orthodox schools of thought. It is divided into Hatha Yoga (the physiological aspect) and Raja (Royal) Yoga (contemplation). The classical account in the Yoga-sūtra of Patanjali includes eight elements or stages: restraint, disciplines, postures, breathing control, elimination of perception of outer objects, concentration, meditation, and absorption. In the Bhagavad Gita, yoga is understood as comprised of three paths that lead to spiritual fulfillment: wisdom or knowledge, action, and ecstatic or loving devotion. While Yoga has its roots in Hinduism, it migrated into other traditions until today you can find yoga centers around the globe that may display any religious or secular (health-oriented lifestyle) purpose.

'Bhakti' is Sanskrit for "devotion." It refers to a devotional movement in Hinduism that flourished in the seventh century in South and in the twelfth and thirteenth centuries in North India. By rejecting the sacrificial ritualism and Brahminical (upper-caste) hegemony of the Vedic tradition, it opened the door for women and members of lower castes to engage in devotional music and dance in pursuit of a mystical union with the divine. Bhakti-yoga is described in the Gita by Krishna:

> The yogi who, established in oneness, Honors Me as abiding in all beings, In whatever way he otherwise acts, Dwells in Me. He who sees equality in everything, In the image of his own Self, Arjuna, Whether in pleasure or in pain, Is thought to be a supreme yogi. Of all yogis, He who has merged his inner Self in Me, Honors me, full of faith, Is thought to be the most devoted to Me.

Hinduism has transitioned over the centuries from being largely ethnic and spread through migration (and marriage) to being spread through widespread, popular teachings and translations of sacred texts. In modern times, the best known Hindu teacher and political activist is Mohandas Gandhi (1869-1948).

Gandhi is best known for leading a massive nonviolent movement for Indian independence from British colonial rule. Gandhi wrote extensively throughout his life. His ninety-seven-volume Collected Works includes valuable reflections on religion, ethics, and philosophy. One of Gandhi's central ideas is the integral relation between means and ends. For Gandhi, the nature of the means is preserved in the nature of the ends. He maintained that one cannot attain peace by violent means, nor can one attain freedom by being subservient. His acts of civil disobedience were part of a life of satyagraha, roughly translated "truth-force," which entails testifying to the fellowship of all humanity by standing firm against forces that divide and oppress. Though a devoted Hindu, Gandhi believed that the same ethical truth could be found in all major religions, that through self-discipline, nonviolence, and devotion to the truth one can live at peace with the world and with other living beings.

Here is a telling passage from Gandhi's *An Autobiography or The Story of My Experiments with Truth*. For Gandhi, the commitment to God, truth, and non-violence were thoroughly integrated. Note, too, his evident humility.

"My uniform experience has convinced me that there is no other God than Truth. And if every page of these chapters does not proclaim to the reader that the only means for the realization of Truth is Ahimsa [the way of nonviolence], I shall deem all my labour in writing these chapters to have been in vain.[...] But this much I can say with assurance, as a result of all my experiments, that a perfect vision of Truth can only follow a complete realization of Ahimsa. To see the universal and all-pervading Spirit of Truth face to face one must be able to love the meanest of creation as oneself. And a man who aspires after that cannot afford to keep out of any field of life. That is why my devotion to Truth has drawn me into the field of politics; and I can say without the slightest hesitation, and yet in all humility, that those who say that religion has nothing to do with politics do not know what religion means. Identification with everything that lives is impossible without self- purification; without self-purification the observance of the law of Ahimsa must remain an empty dream; God can never be realized by one who is not pure of heart. Self-purification therefore must mean purification in all the walks of life. And purification being highly infectious, purification of oneself necessarily leads to the purification of one's surroundings. But the path of self-purification is hard and steep."

Building on this last point, I believe it is Gandhi's free admission that his own imperfections and his own need for self-purification is what gives his writing such power. Indeed, his life itself –with its punishing dimensions of imprisonment and fasting– is a powerful message to us to take his teaching to heart. His giving primacy to truth above all matters is also a stunning testimony of his repudiation of fantasy and falsehood, no matter what the costs.

Gandhi was assassinated by a Hindu nationalist on his way to a prayer meeting on January 30, 1948. He still lives through his teachings and his place in history. Many of his sayings are widespread today. I record six of his dictums. It is worth noting here that all the great teachers of the religions in this immersion coupled their teachings (often recorded by their followers) with memorable, shorter sayings that are instructive for life.

Indeed, in Gandhi's sayings, I suggest that the shorter they are, the greater their content.

> "Live as if you were to die tomorrow. Learn as if you were to live forever."
> "The greatness of humanity is not in being human, but in being humane."
> "In a gentle way, you can shake the world."
> "Change yourself – you are in control."
> "I will not let anyone walk through my mind with their dirty feet."
> "The weak can never forgive. Forgiveness is the attribute of the strong."

Gandhi's writing strongly influenced Martin Luther King. The two did not meet in person (King was 19 years old when Gandhi died), but there is an interesting bond between them. Gandhi was impressed by the teaching of Jesus in the "sermon on the mount" (Gospel of Matthew 5-7) for its teaching on non-violence. He once joked that he did not become a Christian because of other Christians (their hypocrisy and colonialism). And King's commitment to non-violence was forged by a combination of Jesus's teaching and Gandhi's life and practice.

Buddhism

Buddhism emerged from Hinduism, tracing its origin to Siddhartha Gautama, who lived in northern India sometime between the sixth and fourth centuries BCE and came to be known as the Buddha ("Enlightened One"). He was born into an aristocratic family, but he came to renounce his wealthy background when he was confronted with the reality of aging, disease, death, and asceticism. Renouncing his palatial life, Siddhartha pursued many paths to enlightenment using meditation and extreme discipline until, underneath a Bodhi tree, he attained extreme enlightenment. His subsequent teaching centers on The Four Noble Truths.

The Four Noble Truths

These are that: (1) life is full of suffering, pain, and misery; (2) the origin of suffering is in desire; (3) the extinction of suffering can be brought about by the extinction of desire; and (4) the way to extinguish desire is by following the Noble Eightfold Path. The Eightfold Path consists of right understanding; right aspirations or attitudes; right speech; right conduct; right livelihood; right effort; mindfulness; and contemplation or composure.

Early Buddhist teaching tended to be nontheistic, underscoring instead the absence of the self (*anatta*) and the impermanence of life. In its earliest forms, Buddhism did not have a developed metaphysics (that is, a theory of the structure of reality, the nature of space, time, and so on), but did include belief in reincarnation, skepticism about the substantial nature of persons existing over time, and either a denial of the existence of Brahman or the treatment of Brahman as inconsequential. This last stance, along with the denial of the authority of the Vedas, is its clearest departure from Hinduism. The goal of the religious life is *Nirvana*, a transformation of human consciousness that involves the shedding of the illusion of selfhood.

Schools of Buddhism include Theravada Buddhism, the oldest and strictest in terms of promoting the importance of monastic life, Mahayana, which emerged later and displays less resistance to Hindu themes and does not place as stringent an emphasis on monastic vocation, Pure Land Buddhism, and Zen. The most well-known representative of Buddhism throughout the world also needs to be singled out: the current Dalai Lama. Tenzin Gyatso is the 14th Dalai Lama (the name derived from the terms for ocean and teacher, implying one of great wisdom). The Dalai Lamas are believed to be manifestations of Avalokiteshvara or Chenrezig, the Bodhisattva of Compassion and the patron saint of Tibet. He has been the foremost proponent of religious harmony throughout the world. He believes that while it is possible to practice compassion and find happiness outside of religion, the proper function of a fitting religion enhances both compassion and happiness. While, as a Buddhist, he denies that there is a Creator as in the Abrahamic faiths and theistic Hinduism, he does not urge persons of other religions to convert to Buddhism. While he believes that true and everlasting enlightenment is to be found through Buddhist practices, he contends that each person must find fulfillment in the religion that seems most fitting to that person in this life. If a Christian in this life, you may be reborn as a Buddhist in another life to find ultimate enlightenment.

There are, in fact, different understandings of Ultimate Reality within the various streams and schools of Buddhist thought.   In one major Buddhist school, referred to as Madhyamika (school of the 'Middle Way') and developed by Nagarjuna (c.150-c.250 CE), Ultimate Reality is understood to be *sunyata*, which is translated as 'Emptiness' or 'The Void.' It may seem at first glance that 'Emptiness' and Ultimate Reality are contradictory concepts.   How can something fundamentally real be empty or void? But Buddhists of the Madhyamika school (and most schools, in fact) understand 'being real' as 'being independent of other things.'   Fundamental reality, on typical Buddhist metaphysics, is in fact emptiness; there is no 'thing' which has independent existence. All apparent substantial entities, whether galaxies, mountains, trees, or people, are abstractions of events or processes which are dependent on other events or processes.   While such 'things,' including our very selves, appear to be substantial entities, in fact they are not. They seem to be enduring substances, but this is because we abstract from different experiences that occur and then reify substantial entities, including a substantial self, from all of this. Yet they are only processes; in reality, all is in flux. One Buddhist text, in which the following verse is ascribed to The Buddha himself, puts it this way:

> Impermanent are all component things,
> They arise and cease, that is their nature:
> They come into being and pass away,
> Release from them is bliss supreme.

In another writing attributed to The Buddha:

> The five aggregates, monks, are *anicca*, impermanent; whatever is impermanent, that is *dukkha*, unsatisfactory; whatever is dukkha, that is without *attaa*, self. What is without self, that is not mine, that I am not, that is not my self. Thus should it be seen by perfect wisdom (*sammappa~n~naaya*) as it really is. Who sees by perfect wisdom, as it really is, his mind, not grasping, is detached from taints; he is liberated.

Nagarjuna parallels these words: "When the notion of an Atman, Self or Soul cease, the notion of "mine" also ceases and one becomes free from the idea of I and mine."

The Buddha understood the world to be one of transiency, and this is because all discernible entities are in fact composite; all is involved in the fluidity of universal change. Such unstable realities cannot be ultimately real. There is neither Atman nor Brahman, there is no self but Anatman or no-self. In addition, all events and processes originate out of a self-sustaining causal nexus in which each link arises from another, which Buddhists call the doctrine of inter-dependent arising (*ratītyasamutpāda*). All events and processes are connected to other events and processes. Nothing in the nexus is independent; everything arises from something else. By learning this fundamental truth, we are on the path to enlightenment, and on the way to the 'foundation of reality.' On this point, Thich Nhat Hanh writes:

> We have to nourish our insight into impermanence every day. If we do, we will live more deeply, suffer less, and enjoy life much more. Living deeply, we will touch the foundation of reality, nirvana, the world of no-birth and no-death. Touching impermanence deeply, we touch the world beyond permanence and impermanence. We touch the ground of being and see that which we have called being and nonbeing are just notions. Nothing is ever lost. Nothing is ever gained.

One of the causes in the nexus of inter-dependent arising is karma. Because of ignorance (*avidya*), we continue to experience the effects of karma, and this keeps us within the cycle of cause and effect, death, suffering, and rebirth. In order to escape the illusory world of permanence, as Nagarjuna explains it, we need to recognize *sunyata* and so come to see that there are no finite or infinite substances—no individual or permanent selves or beings. It is in this enlightened state that we can ultimately break through the illusion of the phenomenal world, escaping the cycle of death and rebirth and experiencing *Nirvana*, the final extinction of ego and personal desire and an indescribable state of ultimate bliss.

The Buddhist doctrines of *sunyata* and Anatman are not readily apparent to human experience. Why is this so? According to Buddhism, the notions of emptiness, no-self, and the interconnectedness of all things are so distant from our common experience and understanding because we are in desperate need of enlightenment. For Buddhism, the path to enlightenment is the discovery, understanding, and practice of the Four Noble Truths and the Eightfold Path mentioned above.

One important question is how to conceive of rebirth within a Buddhist doctrine of no-self. There is considerable debate among Buddhist scholars on this matter. One common reply is that at the death of consciousness (or the dissolution of the *skandhas*, which, on the Mahayana Buddhist view, are mental events or bundles that constitute what we refer to as the 'ego'), a new consciousness arises, which is rebirth. This new consciousness is not identical to the former, but neither is it completely different from it. There is a causal connection between consciousnesses as they form a part of the same causal continuum. Again, the reason for the belief in an individual substantial self is ignorance (*avidya*). On most Buddhist accounts, in order to move beyond ignorance and to experience enlightenment, one must come to fully understand the central truths, including the truth of Anatman. It is admitted that embracing this teaching may be difficult, and it requires working off the negative effects of karma. Indeed, it will likely require many rebirths to attain full understanding. But it is well worth the effort, Buddhists maintain, for it leads to the *elimination* of suffering and, ultimately, to the eternal bliss of Nirvana.

Buddhist Compassion

'Bodhisattva' is a Sanskrit term that, in Buddhism, refers to a being who is on the way to becoming a Buddha and can enter Nirvana but who remains in this world to spread compassion. Various traditions within Buddhism offer different paths toward release from suffering and enlightenment. The bodhisattva path is one aimed at the highest form of enlightenment (to be a Buddha) and begins with the formation of a compassionate intention to assist all sentient beings. Traditionally, a vow was taken in the presence of a Buddha to enter upon the bodhisattva path. This path includes basic moral purification, meditative practices, and the development of various disciplines until certain non-retrogressive states are reached. Part of the purpose of the path is to accumulate merit, which can then be used to assist all sentient beings. A Bodhisattva, then, is chiefly characterized by compassion for all sentient beings and wisdom to see into the true nature of all reality. They are often seen as compassionate savior figures, particularly in the Mahayana tradition (although they are present in earlier forms of Buddhism as well). Important examples are Maitreya (the Buddha to come), Avalokitesvara (the bodhisattva of compassion—in Tibetan Buddhism the Dalai Lama is an incarnation of this bodhisattva), and Manjusri (the bodhisattva of wisdom).

Senju Kannon (1000-armed Kannon) and the Juichimen Kannon (11-headed Kannon) are different portrayals of the Bodhisattva of Compassion. He is male in India and Tibet, but is usually portrayed as female in China and Japan. There are also many images of Kannon as a single figure without the extra arms or heads. On top of the head of some images of Juichimen Kannon there are 10 heads facing all directions and then one more head (often depicting Amida, the Buddha of Infinite Light and Life). A common explanation is that the 10 heads facing a full 360 degrees symbolize that Kannon can perceive/hear what is going on in all possible directions—and by implication, undifferentiated compassion radiates in all directions to all who might call on Kannon. Another explanation is that each of the 10 heads symbolizes one of the 10 stages of enlightenment. The 25th chapter of the *Lotus Sutra* (the most important and widely used Mahayana Buddhist text in Asia) is devoted to Kannon. Here the name of the bodhisattva is *Perceiver of the World's Sounds*. This name of the bodhisattva (*Perceiver of the World's Sounds*) is Kanzeon in Japanese but it is usually shortened to Kannon. These titles are usually held to mean that this bodhisattva is able to hear and see in all directions any suffering anywhere in the world, and is thus able to be compassionate towards any suffering (from any direction)—and remember, suffering is the fundamental characteristic of this world of birth, life, death, rebirth. Here are the opening lines of chapter 25 of the Lotus Sutra:

> At that time the bodhisattva Inexhaustible Intent immediately rose from his seat, bared his right shoulder, pressed his palms together and, facing the Buddha, spoke these words: "World Honored One, this Bodhisattva Perceiver of the World's Sounds– why is he called Perceiver of the World's Sounds?"

The Buddha said to Bodhisattva Inexhaustible Intent: "Good man, suppose there are immeasurable hundreds, thousands, ten thousands, millions of living beings who are undergoing various trials and suffering. If they hear of this Bodhisattva Perceiver of the Word's Sounds and single-mindedly call his name, then at once he will perceive the sound of their voices and they will all gain deliverance from their trials".

This vision of the Compassionate Buddha has some analogies with theistic tradition and its God of omniscient compassion.

No immersion in Buddhism would be complete without taking note of Zen Buddhism.

Zen Buddhism

Zen originated in China and then spread to Japan and Korea. It became popular in the United States in the mid-twentieth century. There are two forms of Zen, one holding that enlightenment is gradual, the other claiming that enlightenment can be sudden or instantaneous. Zen stresses the goodness of compassion, simplicity, living in the moment, and not getting caught up in abstract discursive reasoning. An influential introduction to Zen is the 1953 book *Zen in the Art of Archery* by Eugene Herrigel. The author goes to Japan to learn of Zen. He discovers that Zen is best approached in a practice like archery, rather than through texts and lectures.

Here is a Zen Master advising Herrigel:

'You cannot do it,' explained the Master, because you do not breathe right. Press your breath down gently after breathing in, so that the abdominal wall is tightly stretched, and hold it there for a while. Then breathe out as slowly and evenly as possible, and, after a short pause, draw a quick breath of air again – out and in continually, in a rhythm that will gradually settle itself. If it is done properly, you will feel the shooting becoming easier every day. For through this breathing you will not only discover the source of all spiritual strength but will also cause this source to flow more abundantly, and to pour more easily through your limbs the more relaxed you are.' And as if to prove it, he drew his strong bow and invited me to step behind him and feel his arm muscles. They were indeed quite relaxed, as though they were doing no work at all.

While I recommend this introduction to Zen for its accessibility (and partly for personal reasons as it had a great impact on me), another text, just as influential and more highly regarded by Zen scholars, is *Zen Mind, Beginner's Mind* by Shunryu Suzuki. Here is a passage that resonates with teaching in the archery text:

> Calmness of mind does not mean you should stop your activity. Real calmness should be found in activity itself. We say, 'It is easy to have calmness in inactivity, it is hard to have calmness in activity, but calmness in activity is true calmness.'

One of the more popular Zen Masters writing in English today is the Vietnamese poet and educator Thich Nhat Hanh. By his lights, enlightened living involves non-violent, natural living. "Drink your tea slowly and reverently, as if it is the axis on which the world earth revolves - slowly, evenly, without rushing toward the future." His writings convey the exquisite joy of being alive when not attached to possessions, the acquisition of wealth, the vice of unprovoked anger.

"People usually consider walking on water or in thin air a miracle. But I think the real miracle is not to walk either on water or in thin air, but to walk on earth. Every day we are engaged in a miracle which we don't even recognize: a blue sky, white clouds, green leaves, the black, curious eyes of a child—our own two eyes. All is a miracle."

The Dalai Lama, referenced several times above, is probably the most well-known living leader of a religion today. His stress on love and compassion has a universal appeal. Consider these four sayings, noting the different ways in which he implores us to follow a minimal ethic of not harming others and then progressing in the quest for the happiness of others and oneself through love.

"Our prime purpose in this life is to help others. And if you can't help them, at least don't hurt them."

"Love and compassion are necessities, not luxuries. Without them, humanity cannot survive."

"If you want others to be happy, practice compassion. If you want to be happy, practice compassion."

"I believe compassion to be one of the few things we can practice that will bring immediate and long-term happiness to our lives. I'm not talking about the short-term gratification of pleasures like sex, drugs or gambling (though I'm not knocking them), but something that will bring true and lasting happiness. The kind that sticks."

No wonder the Dalai Lama is so appreciated today, except perhaps by the Chinese government that does not recognize the independence of the Dalai Lama's homeland of Tibet.

Jainism

Also known as *Jain Dharma*, Jainism is a religion that originated in India toward the end of the Vedic period. Jains believe in a timeless history of endless cosmic cycles. These cycles are divided into two halves: a progressive half and a regressive half. In the third and fourth phases of each half of the cosmic cycle, there are twenty-four Jinas (conquerors) or Tirthankaras (ford-makers). The twenty-fourth Jina of the current cycle was Vardhamana ("increasing"), known as Mahavira ("great hero"), a historical figure who lived near Patna in the state of Bihar and was a contemporary of Siddhartha Guatama.

Mahavira rejected Brahmanism, essentially affirming atheism though it is far from secular atheism. Jains believe that individual persons are indestructible and everlasting. They believe in karma and rebirth. Historians date Mahavira as living from 497 to 425 BCE, but Jain tradition puts him a century earlier, from 599 to 527. Jinas or tirthankaras such as Mahavira in Jainism teach that all living beings, including plants and animals, have an eternal soul. They therefore strictly adhere to the principle of ahimsa, or nonviolence, and undertake many ascetic practices. Jains are strict vegetarians and also avoid root vegetables. The aim of life is to shed one's karma through these ascetic practices and achieve liberation from samsara. By the fifth century CE, Jainism had split into two main sects: one was very strict, holding that no one should own anything, including clothing, while the other was less strict, allowing that some clothing is permissible (white robes) and some possessions were permissible such as an alms bowl, a broom to use to sweep the ground in front of you to prevent your killing insects, and a piece of cloth to wear over your mouth to prevent you destroying life. It is believed that Mahavira took the teaching of non-violence to a radical level when he refused even to eat plants and died of self-starvation at the age of 70.

Overall Mahavira combined the view that all of life involves misfortune and suffering with his teaching about non-violence. So, he says this about birth:

Birth is attended by death, youth by decay and fortune by misfortune. Thus everything in this world is momentary.

And this about the principle of non-violence:

The Arhats [wise teachers who have attained Nirvana] of the past, those of the present and the future narrate thus, discourse thus, proclaim thus, and affirm thus: One should not injure, subjugate, enslave, torture or kill any animal, living being, organism or sentient being. This doctrine of Non-Violence (Ahimsa Dharma) is immaculate, immutable and eternal.

These teachings compel one to see that all life involves suffering, even birth, and that we are called to a higher, purer state.

One of the best known twentieth century advocates of such a radical teaching is the German physician, theologian Albert Schweitzer. He advocated a reverence for life principle. He reasoned that if he reveres his own life, this should be a springboard to revere all of life.

"Ethics thus consists in this, that I experience the necessity of practicing the same reverence for life toward all will-to-live, as toward my own. Therein I have already the needed fundamental principle of morality. It is *good* to maintain and cherish life; it is *evil* to destroy and to check life."

For many of us, Schweitzer's and the Jain's reverence for all of life may seem impractical or even an ideal impossible to follow, but might their ideal still not be an ideal? At a minimum, Schweitzer would implore us to be more compassionate in our treatment of nonhuman animals.

"Wherever any animal is forced into the service of man, the sufferings which it has to bear on that account are the concern of every one of us. No one ought to permit, in so far as he can prevent it, pain or suffering for which he will not take the responsibility. No one ought to rest at ease in the thought that in so doing he would mix himself up in affairs which are not his business. Let no one shirk the burden of his responsibility. When there is so much maltreatment of animals, when the cries of thirsting creatures go up unnoticed from the railway trucks, when there is so much roughness in our slaughter-houses, when in our kitchens so many animals suffer horrible deaths from unskilful hands, when animals endure unheard-of agonies from heartless men, or are delivered to the dreadful play of children, then we are all guilty and must bear the blame."

Albert Schweitzer's reverence for life principle is often included in textbooks in environmental ethics as representative of Jain values.

Confucianism

Confucius (in Chinese, Kongfuzi, "Revered Master Kong") (551–479 BCE) was born during the Spring and Autumn Period, when China was politically divided and the Zhou dynasty was declining. The *Analects* (in Chinese, lunyu, "conversations") is a compilation of his teachings, often in a dialogue format, collected by his student-disciples. Confucius sought to revitalize Li (rites), reverence for Heaven, honor for ancestors, and the self-cultivation of virtue. He maintained that our humanity (Ren) is naturally oriented to virtue and self-restraint in the family and community. Confucius expressed the basic principle of human interaction as follows: "When we seek to have ourselves established, we also seek to establish others; when we seek to have ourselves fulfilled, we also seek to fulfill others." Reciprocity (in Chinese, lin) was central. Although Confucius assumed a ruler would inherit his position from his father, he also argued that a ruler's legitimacy necessarily depends on his ruling morally. As the purpose of government is to promote the subjects' welfare, a ruler should serve as a moral exemplar for his subjects. Confucius has generally been viewed as a conservative, not introducing radically new institutions but repairing and renewing older traditions. While revered as a great sage teacher, there is reason to see his chief aim in life was to reduce the suffering (and warfare) among Chinese. His teaching of young men has been seen as him preparing the next generation to promote just rulership in ways that he himself as an individual had failed to do in his lifetime.

Overall, Confucianism is a moral, social, religious, and political philosophy originating in China that has also profoundly shaped Japan, Korea, and Vietnam. I have included Confucianism in this immersion into religions because it has enough features falling under our definition of religion (and it is recognized as a religion by the American Academy of Religion), but some would classify if more as a philosophy than a religion. There are Confucian temples but these may also be seen more as monuments than places of worship. Still, Confucius is believed to have engaged in such religious-like practices as praying, attending sacrifices, fasting, and counsels that his followers should "stand in awe of the ordinances of Heaven."

Over many years Confucianism was enforced by the civil service examination system, the principal means of recruiting government officials from the seventh century to 1905, when the Confucian civil service examinations were abolished.

Confucian Wisdom

Because so much of the teaching of Confucius is a compilation of his followers, we may see his work as the work of multiple persons seeking to further expand his themes of the importance of humility, education, awareness of one's role in family and community, the importance of rites and ethical self-cultivation. The teachings attributed to Confucius, like the other key figures in the religions of the world (like Buddha and Jesus) are often encapsulated in easy to memorize form.

"Before you embark on a journey of revenge, dig two graves."

"Real knowledge is to know the extent of one's ignorance."

"Do not do to others what you do not want done to yourself."

"It is easy to hate and it is difficult to love. This is how the whole scheme of things works. All good things are difficult to achieve; and bad things are very easy to get."

"Respect yourself and others will respect you."

These sayings border on common sense; indeed, Confucius is often understood as seeking to restore an older moral order. They have dramatic weight, however, when you take into account that

Confucius lived during a time of great suffering and political turmoil. His teaching about respecting others was launched when there was very little respect for others.

The most important follower of Confucius was Mencius (fourth century BCE). 'Mencius' is the Latinized form of Mengzi (Master Meng). After Confucius himself, he is the most important philosopher of the classical era. Arguing against the Legalist school, which held that human beings are basically amoral and motivated by self-interest, Mencius claimed everyone is born with a predisposition to the good. This predisposition, however, must be cultivated through education and example. By his lights, four significant moral virtues emerge from within: humanity, righteousness, propriety, and wisdom. Mencius taught that any person might become a sage through education and self-cultivation.

Here is one of Mencius's famous sayings in which he advances his view that it is human nature to tend toward goodness.

"It is true that water will flow indifferently to east and west, but will it flow equally well up and down? Human nature is disposed toward goodness, just as water tends to flow downwards. There is no water but flows downwards, and no man but shows his tendency to be good. Now, by striking water hard, you may splash it higher than your forehead, and by damming it, you may make it go uphill. But, is that the nature of water? It is external force that causes it to do so. Likewise, if a man is made to do what is not good, his nature is being similarly forced."

Mencius taught that the path toward goodness had to involve charity or compassion.

"Charity is in the heart of man, and righteousness in the path of men. Pity the man who has lost his path and does not follow it and who has lost his heart and does not know how to recover it. When people's dogs and chicks are lost they go out and look for them and yet the people who have lost their hearts do not go out and look for them. The principle of self-cultivation consists in nothing but trying to look for the lost heart."

Because Mencius thought our nature inclines us to the good, his approach to education was more gentle than teachers who thought their students were naturally bent to wrong-doing and required harsh, disciplinary correction. The following dialogue between Mencius and Kao Tzu (c420-350 BCE) is instructive. Kao Tzu believed that education needed to correct human nature and inclinations.

"Kao Tzu said, 'Human nature is like the willow tree, and righteousness is like a cup or a bowl. To turn human nature into humanity and righteousness is like turning the willow tree into cups and bowls.' Mencius said, 'Sir, can you follow the nature of the willow tree and make the cups and bowls, or must you violate the nature of the willow tree before you can make the cups and bowls? If you are going to violate the nature of the willow tree in order to make cups and bowls, then you must also violate human nature in order to make it into humanity and righteousness? Your words, alas, would lead people in the world to consider humanity and righteousness as calamity.'"

Mencius's more positive view of humanity and education calls to mind a story about Anselm of Canterbury. It is said that he was approached by a school teacher who complained about his unruly student. The teacher reported that once he corrected their behavior by harsh discipline they became utterly boring. Anselm instructed the teacher to be less harsh and give the students more freedom. Anselm, like Mencius, trusted in the good nature of students, even if this is not always obvious!

An important rival to Confucianism is Mohism, a religious-philosophical tradition believed to have been launched by Motzi (sometimes spelled Mo Tzu) who lived in the fifth and fourth century BCE in China. In contrast with Confucianism with its foundation in particular relationships (parent-child, and so on), Mohism espouses universal love. Here is an example of how this would play out: Imagine you are the head of an army of 100 soldiers facing an opposing army of 100 soldiers. You are forced to choose between two plans that are highly likely to lead to your victory: plan A will result in the death of 10 of your soldiers and 80 deaths in the opposing army;

plan B will involve the death of 40 of your soldiers and 40 of the enemy. From a Moist point of view, you should choose plan B, because from the standpoint of loving all persons you should do that act that would involve fewer deaths.

Here is a Mohist argument I find intriguing. Imagine you have to leave your mother in the care of some other persons. Would you choose to leave your mother with a follower of Confucius or Motzi? Evidently, the Mohist who crafted this question thought the natural answer would be to leave your mother with a Mohist. But I myself am hesitant about this. The follower of Confucius would appreciate the particular importance of the concrete case of your love for your mother, while the Mohist may be so focused on universal love that they are less keenly focused on the particular relationship at stake. I leave the matter up to you.

Daoism

Laozi (c. sixth century) or "the Old Master" is believed to be the author of the Daodejing (also spelled Tao Te Ching), and the founder of Daoism (sometimes spelled Taoism). Daoism originated in China and then spread to Japan, Korea, and Vietnam.

The Daodejing evokes a Dao ("Way"), an ultimate reality that cannot be described in language or through rational discourse, but can only be grasped intuitively. Using indirect language, particularly paradox and analogy, the Daodejing suggests that there is a natural order in the universe and that wise persons seek to adapt and respond to that natural order. Passivity and humility are virtues. Water, for example, is soft and yielding yet able to wear down stone. The Daodejing rejects the Confucian stress on ritual, propriety, and moral self-cultivation. Its ideal of "non-action," extoles simple, natural behavior. There is a Dao to most activities from being a wise ruler to being a butcher to having sex. Living in harmony with nature is the key.

In essence, the Dao refers to the processes of life which flow back and forth in a correlative pattern between yin and yang, the receptive and the active, in which elements that seem to be contrary or contradictions are often complementary. Daoism does not uphold a strict dualism between good and evil that one finds in the Abrahamic tradition, nor a Confucian concept of a good nature, but they do see tyrants, oppressive forces, and cruelty as contrary to the Dao. A wise ruler –who would impose minimal constraints— rules in accord with the Dao.

While the followers of Confucius tended to be rule-following, conformists who stress responsibility, hierarchy, service, and seriousness, Daoists value individuality, non-conformity, tranquility, and wit.

The Mystery of the Dao

Here are the famous opening lines of the Daodejing:

The Dao that can be spoken is not the eternal Dao

The name that can be named is not the eternal name

The nameless is the origin of Heaven and Earth

The named is the mother of myriad things

Thus, constantly without desire, one observes its essence

Constantly with desire, one observes its manifestations

These two emerge together but differ in name

The unity is said to be the mystery

Mystery of mysteries, the door to all wonders

Religion and Eastern Cultures

Daoism, Buddhism, and Confucianism are tolerated in China since the establishment of the People's Republic of China in 1949, as are groups practicing indigenous or folk religion, Christianity (estimated as 2.53% of the population) and Islam (.45% - 2.85%), albeit under close supervision/monitoring, as Mao Zedong fostered the Marxist notion that religions are feudal. China has an official policy of state atheism. In the Chinese constitution, article 36 guarantees limited freedom of religion so long as these are officially sanctioned by the state.

How secular is contemporary China? The sociologist of religion, Rodney Stark, contends that it all depends on how one defines "religion" and "being secular." It is estimated that 75% of Chinese today claim to have no religion. Stark responds:

"But the fact is that most of them [the 75%] frequently visit temples where they pray to various statues of gods and offer them gifts of food, and 72% of those who said they had no religion said they had engaged in ancestor worship during the past year."

It turns out that if by "religion" one means being a formal member of a church or temple or mosque and so on, few Chinese are religious, but matters change if religion covers reverential venerations, invoking the supernatural, and so on. Stark observes:

"In the past thirty years after several decades of severe repression, religion has been springing up everywhere in China. Tens of thousands of temples have been reopened or rebuilt. Millions have returned to Buddhism, and once again huge numbers of Chinese are pursuing their traditional folk religions and worshipping at their ancestral shrines."

In this sense, Daniel Overmyer (University of British Columbia) writes:

"Wherever local conditions permit, religious activities come bubbling to the surface, festivals to the gods are held, traditional funerals and burial rituals are restored, destroyed images and shrines are replaced, priests appear to perform rituals, and congregations meet to worship."

Some mention of Taiwan is fitting as it has a general reputation for being secular. It turns out only 18% of the Taiwan population claim to have no religion, while 35% self-identify as Buddhist, 33% as Daoists, 8% align with folk religion, 4% as Christian, and 2% a medley of religions (e.g. 60,000 Muslims, 51,000 Mormons, and so on).

The five religious-philosophical traditions in this chapter often generated important dialectical encounters historically. In India, there were recurring debates between Hindu and Buddhist philosophers. When Islam came to India, the realm of debate grew even larger. In China, imperial courts sometimes sponsored extended symposia when the different Chinese religions and philosophies were given hearings.

In the last chapter we looked at the Abrahamic faiths in global perspective. What are some of the effects of the great religions we have immersed ourselves in for these Eastern traditions? For those countries impacted by Confucianism the family is often considered a central focus of life. Governments tend to be paternal and centralized. In light of Confucius and Mencius teaching about goodness and education, it is often assumed (in China and elsewhere) that each child can benefit from education. Along these lines, it should be noted that China has one of the highest literacy rates in the world, 96.84% (the global rate is 86.3%). The diversity of religions in India has led to government that is less centralized than in China. The general outlook that we should live in harmony with nature (found in Daoism and Confucianism) has contributed to a climate in which different religions can flourish in co-existence. In Japan, Shintoism (to be addressed in the next chapter), Buddhism, and Confucianism have been seen as equally valid spiritual paths. In Japan it is not uncommon for people to celebrate Christmas on December 25, to engage in a Buddhist rite on New Year's Eve, and to visit a Shinto shrine on New Year's day. It is not unusual for weddings in Japan to have a Christian-style and about 90% of the funerals in Japan use Buddhist rites. I do not suggest that following these rites (even child-dedications on Shinto shrines) are motivated by beliefs in the truth of these different, religious worldviews, but they are some evidence of the affective appeal of these religious modes of life.

For readers with interests in business, it should be noted that some attribute the economic growth of Japan, South Korea, Singapore, and Taiwan to a work ethic that has its roots in Confucianism. Arguably, some of the formalities of social interactions seem to echo Confucianism.

At the end of the last chapter I raised three questions readers may have about the Abrahamic faiths concerning the intellectual respectability of theism, the relationship of God and ethics, and the problem of evil. The Asian religious-philosophical traditions are so diverse that they do not lend themselves easily to such questions. As for theism, there are theistic elements in Hinduism but if you are a non-theist, Buddhism and Jainism are non-theistic. On the role of ethics in the religions in this chapter, some Hindu sacred texts have divinely revealed precepts, but many do not (Buddhism, Confucianism, Jainism, Daoism). Speaking very generally, ethics in Asian traditions have historically involved some tension between giving primacy to family and community versus the individual and monastic life. But what might be described as tension may also be thought of in terms of a plurality of values, without prioritizing one over the other (e.g. not advocating that it is better to be a parent than a celibate monk). As for the problem and the very concept of evil, there are myriad views. Today, there is a widespread acknowledgement of human rights and international law throughout Asia, but obviously (as in the rest of the world) this is profoundly either not practiced or not acknowledged in regions where there is persecution, oppression, and (unjust) occupation. In some of the religious traditions originating in Asia, evil is more a matter of ignorance rather than the willful sin against the Creator.

In the next chapter, let us consider three more religious traditions and then consider whether the diversity of religions in the world should be thought of as healthy or as a problem.

Chapter 4

More Religions and Religious Pluralism

As noted at the outset of this book, the vast majority of the world population is religious. The last chapter briefly referenced the secular atheism of Mao, but even Maoism has had quasi-religious features: Mao is considered in Messianic terms, his sayings are deemed sacred, his body is preserved for veneration (or at least as a site for admiration of the founder of the People's Republic). Peter Berger, like many of his fellow sociologists, once predicted that religion would wither in contemporary life. He utterly changed his prediction. He now contends that "the real situation is that most of the world is as religious as it ever was. You have enormous explosions of religion in the world... In fact, you can say every major religious tradition has been going through a period of resurgence in the last 30, 40 years or so... anything but secularization."

Is the growth and diversity of religions a problem? One might not think so; after all, with more diverse ways of seeing reality and responding to the sacred, might it be the case that the more choices we have, the more likely that one or more of these worldviews is true? And yet some wonder whether this diversity is a sign that one should be agnostic. After all, it seems that equally intelligent, sensitive persons may be Christians or Buddhists or Hindus and so on. Before taking on this question, let us pause to note three more significant religious worldviews and practices that we have not covered yet: Sikhism, Shintoism, and the Bahai. These are especially interesting as Sikhism sought to meld elements of Hinduism and Islam, whereas Shintoism is a broadly religious or spiritual movement that may be especially interesting today for readers with environmental interests. While Shintoism is geographically centered in Japan with little presence in, say, Europe and America (apart from some global Japanese companies having Shinto shrines in their buildings), it is representative in this guide as akin to the spirituality of indigenous and native persons elsewhere who see the natural world as sacred.

Sikhism

Sikhism emerged in the Punjab region of India in the 1500s, based on the teachings of the Guru Nanak (1469–1538). The name "Sikh" itself means "disciple" or "learner." Sikhism is monotheistic; it views God as the One, the Truth, the omnipresent Creator. It rejects idolatry and belief in incarnations, but it recognizes reincarnation, karma, and the Hindu view of samsara. Initially committed to nonviolence or pacifism, it evolved to include military service. Virtues include truth-telling, justice, impartiality, gratitude. It rejects the caste system, wine, pilgrimages, tobacco. There are successive stages of life from wrong-doing to the eventual attainment of union with God, eternal bliss and freedom from re-birth. After receiving a revelation from God, Nanak made long trips to spread his teaching and to set up religious centers in India and Arabia.

Sikhs view religious diversity as a gift from God, understanding different forms of worship and religious traditions as contextual articulations of the one universal truth. In the Dasam Granth, Guru Gobind Singh wrote, "Recognize all human kind, whether Muslim or Hindu as one. The same God is the Creator and Nourisher of all. Recognize no distinction among them. The temple and the mosque are the same. So are Hindu worship and Muslim prayer. Human beings are all one." Sikhs welcome non-Sikhs to communal meals at Sikh temples. They welcome persons, male and female, from all castes and nationalities.

Today, there are about twenty million Sikhs in the world, most of whom live in the Punjab region of India.

Consider two sacred texts. The first testified to monotheism:

> There is one God,
> Eternal Truth is His name;
> Maker of all things,
> Fearing nothing and at enmity with nothing,
> Timeless is His Image;
> Not begotten, being of His own Being;
> By the grace of thee Guru, made known to man.

In this second passage there is a celebration of qudrat, the Arabic term for what is created or natural, along with a recognition of the sacred nature of the holy books of other religions.

> What we see is the One's qudrat,
> What we hear is the One's qudrat,
> Qudrat is at the core of happiness and fear,
> The skies, the nether regions and all that is visible is the one's qudrat
> The Vedas, the Purans, the Quran, indeed all that is thought is qudrat,
> Eating, drinking, dressing up is qudrat, so is all love qudrat!

You may recognize male Sikhs by their turbans to protect their hair. They consider their hair a gift from God and they thereby keep their hair uncut and well groomed.

Shintoism

Shintoism or Shinto, from the Sino-Japanese shin (gods) and tō (way or dao) –sometimes translated as "the way of the gods"– refers to the indigenous religion that existed in Japan before the introduction of Buddhism and has coexisted with Buddhism to the present. It has no founder, creed, or sacred scripture. It is polytheistic and involves worship or veneration of spirits throughout the natural world as well as ancestors. All great works of nature —waterfalls, huge trees, unusual rocks, and so on— are kami or sacred beings. Kami does not mean "god" or divinity in the Western sense, but suggests awesomeness and special powers.

Shinto was the official religion of Japan from 1871 to 1945 with the defeat of the Japanese in World War II. Emperor Hirohito was regarded as a god, from a Shinto perspective, who was compelled in a peace treaty to announce he was not divine. It is estimated that today there are 100,000 Shinto shrines in Japan and 20,000 priests.

Because the veneration of the natural world is at the heart of the Shinto worldview it is especially attractive to those who are environmentally oriented.

There is a revived interest in Shinto with the emergence in Western philosophy of pan-psychism, according to which the foundational elements of the physical world have some psychic dimension.

The Bahai Faith

Bahai faith is monotheistic; it holds that God is omnipresent, omniscient, almighty, and eternal. The Bahai faith or religion began in the nineteenth century in Persia and spread initially in the Middle East. It teaches the unity of all religions. "Bahai" is from the Arabic Bah á, meaning "glory" or "splendor." Bahais believe that God's will has been progressively revealed through a variety of messengers (including Abraham, Krishna, Buddha, Moses, Jesus, Muhammad, Zoroaster, and so on), the most recent of whom is Bah á 'u'll á h. The Bahai faith claims that God, in his very essence, is incomprehensible, but becomes manifested in different forms at different times and places. The Bahai are fiercely critical of nationalism, racism, and religious wars.

The Bahai view that religions are (at their deepest level) different views of the same God is based, in part, on their view that the essence of God far transcends human knowing. This is essential as it allows the Bahai to see the religions of the world as pointing to God, but only reflecting some aspect of the transcendence of God.

To every discerning and illumined heart it is evident that God, the unknowable Essence, the divine Being, is immensely exalted beyond every human attribute...Far be it from His glory that human tongue should adequately recount His praise, or that human heart comprehend His fathomless mystery.

(*The Kitáb-i-Íqán*)

For the Bahai, the diversity of religions in the world is a gift.

The door of the knowledge of the Ancient of Days being thus closed in the face of all beings, the Source of infinite grace...hath caused those luminous Gems of Holiness to appear out of the realm of the spirit, in the noble form of the human temple, and be made manifest unto all men, that they may impart unto the world the mysteries of the unchangeable Being, and tell of the subtleties of His imperishable Essence.

(*The Kitáb-i-Íqán*)

It is estimated that there are five million Bahai today.

So, is diversity a problem?

The philosopher John Hospers suggests that it is. He lists the names of forty gods that seem to have disappeared without a trace from human history (none of them treated in this book). Consider three possible responses: religious pluralism, exclusivism and harmony in diversity.

Religious pluralism: One response would be to claim that all religions point to a common end, the sacred or an Ultimate Reality or what one famous religious pluralist (John Hick) calls the Real. This has some allegiance with a Bahai perspective. The diversity of religions offer different paths to the same end, just as there might be different trails on a mountain. This is a reasonable account, though we have seen some incompatible claims among different religions –the affirmation that there is a God, a creator (in the Abrahamic faiths, theistic Hinduism, and Sikhism, and in the Bahai faith) and the denial that there is a God (Buddhism, Jainism). Still, John Hick proposes that all the religious faiths are experiences in different ways of the Real that is beyond human experience. The Real is, as it were, *the Real in itself,* whereas the different religions are what we take as real for us. In a range of publications over thirty years, Hick advocated what he described as a Copernican revolution in religion. Just as Copernicus advocated a sun-centered view of our planets, Hick advocated a Real-centered view of religions. As the sun may be seen from each of the eight planets in our solar system, the religions of the world may be viewed (partially) from the religions of the world. The comparison with Copernicus is fitting, though the Real (according to Hick) cannot be grasped directly –so it is not quite like seeing the sun from different angles. The Real is not in itself knowable; it may only be mediated by way of different religions. Hick refers to the Real as a "divine noumenon" –something we postulate but cannot directly experience. In his important book, *An Interpretation of Religion: Human Responses to the Transcendent*, Hick writes:

"But if the Real in itself is not and cannot be humanly experienced, why postulate such an unknown and unknowable *Ding an sich* [German for 'thing in itself']? The answer is that the divine noumenon is a necessary postulate of the pluralistic religious life of humanity. For within each tradition we regard as real the object of our worship or contemplation. If… it is also proper to regard as real the objects of worship or contemplation within the other traditions, we are led to postulate the Real *an sich* as the presupposition of the veridical character of this range of forms of religious experience. Without this postulate we should be left with a plurality of personae and impersonae each of which is claimed to be the Ultimate, but no one of which alone can be. We should have either to regard all the reported experiences as illusory or else return to the confessional position in which we affirm the authenticity of our own stream of religious experience whilst dismissing as illusory those occurring within other traditions. But for those to whom neither of these options seems realistic the pluralistic affirmation becomes inevitable, and with it the postulation of the Real *an sich*, which is variously experienced and thought..."

Pluralism thereby seeks to affirm that all the main religions are valid both in terms of justification (persons of intellectual integrity are all warranted in their beliefs and practices) and in their portal (vantage point in revering) to what lies beyond all human vision, the Real.

Another way to endorse a kind of pluralism is to hold that the collective religious experiences of most of humanity is not enough to justify an exclusive adherence to one religion, but it would be enough evidence to think that secular naturalism or physicalism (there is only what the physical sciences describe and explain) is false. Tim Mawson adopts this position:

"The commonalities among people's religious experiences -and here we must remember to include those of the adherents of religions that do not see the supernatural order as personal- is merely that there is some supernatural realm; that it is not malevolent; and that putting oneself in touch with it is of vital importance. As such, the collective testimony of humanity is not enough to give us positive reason to prefer one religion over any other.

Even then, though, it does give us reason to suppose that physicalism is false."

Exclusivism: One may argue that one religion is true and the others are (in some measure) false. The qualification "in some measure" is needed for if any one of the main religions addressed in this book is true, then there are truths in other religions. For example, all religions I have studied on all the continents of this planet include some version of the Golden Rule, some teaching on the good of compassion and the ill or vice of greed, being selfish and cruel. So, what may be called "exclusivism" needs to be seen as not an all or nothing matter. If the Bahai faith or Sikhism are true, large parts of all other religions are true.

A common core of religious experience?

Without going all the way with John Hick's pluralism, Caroline Davis has identified a "common core" of six beliefs and experiences across most religions. This list is taken from her book The Evidential Force of Religious Experience:

(i) The mundane world of physical bodies, physical processes, and narrow centres of consciousness is not the whole or ultimate reality.

(ii) There is a far deeper "true self" which in some way depends on and participates in the ultimate reality.

(iii) Whatever is the ultimate reality is holy, eternal, and of supreme value; it can appear to be more truly real than all else, since everything else depends on it.

(iv) This holy power can be experienced as an awesome, loving, pardoning, guiding presence with whom individuals can have a personal relationship.

(v) ...at least some mystical experiences are experiences of a very intimate union with the holy power...

(vi) Some kind of union or harmonious relation with the ultimate reality is the human being's summum bonum [highest good], his final liberation or salvation, and the means by which he discovers his "true self" or "true home."

Harmony in diversity: One may argue that there are many complementary goods and truths among the diverse religions of the world. So, unlike religious pluralism, this option might lead a Christian to think God is Triune and became incarnate as Jesus, and yet believe that (for example) Muslims devotion to Allah, the Buddhist stress on compassion, the care for the natural world in Shintoism, and so on, exceeds the devotion, compassion, and environmental sensitivity of ordinary Christians.

The Christian Archbishop Desmond Tutu appears to take this third position. Without denying his belief in the Lordship of Jesus Christ, he stresses the unity of all persons and our (that is, everyone) shared calling to pursue goodness and love.

"It doesn't matter where we worship or what we call God; there is only one, inter-dependent human family. We are born for goodness, to love – free of prejudice. All of us, without exception. There is greater commonality in our belief systems than we tend to credit, a golden thread expressed in the maxim that one should treat others as one would like others to treat oneself. I don't believe in the notion of "opposing belief systems." It would be more accurate to say that human beings have a long history of rationalizing acts of inhumanity on the basis of their own interpretations of the will of God."

In a recent interview, Tutu says:

"Our failure to recognize the humanity in others lays the foundations for selfishness rather than selflessness. It leads to gross inequity and hideous disparities in qualities of life – and, often, the degradation of environments in which relatively poor people live. A world that recognizes the equal worth and vulnerabilities of all its people will be a much more peaceful place."

I hope you have enjoyed this immersion into some of the great religions of the world. I hope (and pray) this will only be the beginning or your exploring the awesome, living religions that we may encounter today.

Further Reading

Alston, William. (1991). *Perceiving God.* Ithaca: Cornell University, Press.

Buber, Martin (1970) *I and Thou.* New York: Scribner.

Eck, Diana. (1993). *Encountering God.* Boston: Beacon Press.

Evans, C. Stephen. (2010). *Natural Signs and Knowledge of God.* Oxford: Oxford University Press.

Harrison, Victoria. (2019) *Eastern Philosophy: The Basics,* second edition. London: Routledge.

Hick, John. (2006). *The New Frontier of Religion and Science.* New York: Palgrave Macmillan

Kwan, Kai-Man. (2011). *The Rainbow of Experiences, Critical Trust, and God; A Defense of Holisitic Empiricism.* London: Continuum Press.

Maslow, Abraham H. (1970). *Religions, Values, and Peak-Experiences.* New York: The Viking Press.

Mawson, T. J. (2005). *Belief in God.* Oxford: Oxford University Press.

Meister, Chad (ed). (2010). *The Oxford Handbook of Religious Diversity*. Oxford: Oxford University Press.

Prothero, Stephen. (1993). *God is Not One; The Eight Revival Religions that run the world -and why their differences matter*. Boston: Beacon Press.

Robinson, Thomas. (2014). *World Religions; A Guide to the Essentials*. Ada, MI: Baker.

Smart, Ninian. (1960). *A Dialogue of Religions*. London: SCM.

Smith, Huston. (2009). *The World's Religions*. San Francisco: HarperOne.

Smith, Huston (1995). *The Illustrated World's Religions*. San Francisco: HarperOne.

Stark, Rodney (2007). *Discovering God: The Origins of the Great Religions and the Evolution of Belief*. San Francisco: HarperOne.

Stark, Rodney. (2015). *The Triumph of Faith. Why the World Is More Religious Than Ever*. Wilmington, DE: ISI Books.

Taliaferro and Meister, Chad. (2016). *Contemporary Philosophical Theology*. New York: Routledge, 2016.

Taliaferro, Charles and Evans, Jil. (2021). *Is God Invisible? An Essay on Religion and Aesthetics*. Cambridge: Cambridge University Press.

Ward, Keith. (2000). *Religion and Community*. Oxford: Clarendon Press.

Ward, Keith. (2006). *Is Religion Dangerous?* Grand Rapids: Eerdmans.

Chronology
Figures and events in the history of religion from the beginning to the early twentieth century

(c.= circa, signifying approximate dates)

c. 2600 BCE Indus Valley Civilization

c. 1812–c. 1637, though some date at 2,000 BCE Abraham

c. 1500–c. 1200 BCE Development of Brahmanism. Likely composition of Hindu Vedas.

c. 1300 BCE Moses and the Ten Commandments

c. 1000 BCE Kingdom of Israel begins

c. 1000–500 BCE Pentateuch is written

c. 800–400 BCE Likely composition of early Hindu Upanishads

c. 600–583 BCE Zoroaster (Zarathustra), founder of Zoroastrianism in Persia

c. 599–527 BCE Mahāvīra, founder of Jainism

586–587 BCE Babylonians conquer Jerusalem; Israelites taken into captivity

c. 570–510 BCE Laozu, founder of Daoism

c. 566–486 BCE Siddhartha Gautama (Buddha), founder of Buddhism

c. 551–479 BCE Confucius, founder of Confucianism

531 BCE Siddhartha attains Enlightenment

c. 500 BCE Emergence of Shintoism in Japan, though probably earlier

c. 469–399 BCE Socrates

427–347 BCE Plato

384–322 BCE Aristotle

c. 372–289 BCE Mencius, Confucian philosopher

221 BCE Great Wall of China built

206 BCE–220 CE Han Dynasty

200–100 BCE Buddhism splits into Theravada and Mahayana

c. 4 BCE–c. 30 CE Jesus of Nazareth, founder of Christianity

c. 150–200 Nagarjuna, founder of Madhyamaka school of Buddhism

c. 215–276 Mani, founder of Manichaeism

325 Council of Nicaea

354–430 St. Augustine of Hippo 3

80 Christianity becomes the official religion of the Roman Empire

410 Fall of Rome

570–632 Muhammad, prophet of Islam

610 Muhammad receives his first revelation from God in a cave during Ramadan 613 Muhmmad begins preaching about his revelations

c. 650 Qur'an written

c. 788–c. 820 Adi Shankar, founder of Advanta Vedanta Hinduism

789 Beginning of the Viking Expansion

c. 801–866 Al-Kindī; 859 Founding of the first university, University of Karueein, Fez, Morocco

870–950 Al-Farabi

962 The Holy Roman Empire is established

980–1037 Avicenna

1017–1137 Ramanuja

1033–1109 St. Anselm of Canterbury

1059–1111 Al-Ghazali

1079–1142 First Crusade

1099 Christian capture of Jerusalem

1126–1198 Averroes

1135–1204 Moses Maimonides

c. 1181–1226 St. Francis of Assisi

1200 Sacking and burning of Library of Nalanda

1221–1327 Mongol Invasion of India

1225–1274 Thomas Aquinas

1254–1324 Marco Polo

1258 Sack of Baghdad

1346–1353 The Black Plague

1453 Constantinople falls to the Ottomans, ending the Byzantine era

1483–1546 Martin Luther

1492 Columbus' Voyage; expulsion of the Jews from Spain

1509–1564 John Calvin

1517 Luther nails his 95 Theses to the castle church door in Wittenberg, Germany 1517–1648 The Reformation

1813–1855 Kierkegaard

1815 End of the Napoleonic Wars

1817–1892 Bahaullah, founder of the Bhai

1818–1883 Karl Marx

1921 Consolidation of the foundation of the Bhai faith

Quick Immersion Series

For more information, please follow us on Facebook @TibidaboPublishing or visit www.quickimmersions.com

Made in the USA
Monee, IL
30 October 2021